P9-DBJ-717

BALLANTINE BOOKS / NEW YORK

in the
kitchen
with DAVID

QVC'S RESIDENT FOODIE Presents
COMFORT FOODS
that take you HOME

DAVID VENABLE

foreword by Paula Deen

Published in the United States by Ballantine Books, an imprint of The Random House Publishing Group,
a division of Random House, Inc., New York.

BALLANTINE and colophon are registered trademarks of Random House, Inc.

Some of the recipes in this work were originally featured on *In the Kitchen with David* on QVC.

Photographs by Ben Fink Photography, Inc.

ISBN 978-0-345-53628-0

eISBN 978-0-345-53629-7

Printed in the United States of America on acid-free paper

www.ballantinebooks.com

246897531

First Edition

Book design by Susan Turner

For my mother, Sarah,

you taught me how to cook
and how to dream

contents

foreword

A BOOMING VOICE called out, "Is there a Paula Deen here?"

That's how I met David Venable. It was 1998, and I was in the QVC prep kitchen, whipping up some last-minute biscuits and checking other dishes before heading to the set. I was there to sell my very first book, *The Lady & Sons Savannah Country Cookbook.*

I popped up from behind a table, covered from head to elbows in flour. Standing before me was this unbelievably tall man with a grin as wide as the Mississippi. I looked him square in the eyes and asked, "Are you David?" His grin got even wider. "That's me."

"Do you understand Southern food?"

"Yes, ma'am. I do. I was born and raised in North Carolina. I know my grits. I know biscuits."

I stood on my tippy toes and gave David the world's biggest hug. Well, I forgot that I was all dusted and floured up. That hug made us both look like we were ready for the skillet. We were so excited when we finally got on the air that night that we told our how-we-met story to viewers and couldn't stop sharing our memories of cooking and eating authentic Southern food. (I was so thrilled and surprised when my book sold out in mere minutes!) David and I have been the best of friends ever since.

I've been lucky enough to be on *In the Kitchen with David,* eating, tasting, laughing, misbehaving, and carrying on, more times than I can count. And I'm sure y'all know that man does love his food. I am so delighted that he has put together a collection of his favorite recipes, because now y'all get to be *In the Kitchen with David* just like I do. And y'all are going to love David, his cooking, and his energy just as much as I do.

—*Paula Deen*

introduction

HELLO, FOODIES!

It's just moments before airtime on QVC's *In the Kitchen with David,* and I'm putting the finishing touches on my recipe demonstrations for today's show. As I look over the table filled with my ingredients and prepared dishes, I can't help but smile at how lucky I am to be able to share my lifelong love of great food with my viewers.

I'm a Southern boy, born and raised in Charlotte, North Carolina, and I love good eating. Even as a kid, I always looked forward to mealtime with a sense of celebration. I come from a family of accomplished cooks, so when the Venables get together, we eat and eat plenty! My love of cooking was born out of my desire to make, enjoy, and remember all the favorite foods of my childhood, from chicken and dumplings to chicken-fried steak to coconut layer cake.

Having been taught to cook by my mom and grandmothers, I learned to achieve balance in my recipes and meals. Mom insisted that our dinner plates have a main course and two side dishes. She taught me to respect and create food with layers of flavor by adding some fresh herbs or a few strips of crumbled bacon. She believed cooking would be a skill that would benefit me for the rest of my life. As always, Mom was right.

As my skills in the kitchen improved, I came to understand that cooking should never feel like a chore. The whole process, from prepping the food to the cooking to sitting down at the table, should be easy, creative, and joyful. I became a better cook by eating in restaurants, trying unfamiliar dishes, and asking lots of questions. I took all that new information home with me. When family recipes like smothered pork chops or buttermilk biscuits were already perfect, I didn't change a thing. But I jumped right in when it came to trying new ingredients or techniques or improving my macaroni and cheese or elevating my chili to ultimate status. For me, comfort food is all of these things—old favorites and new classics.

I've come to realize that comfort food isn't limited to the South. No matter where we live or where our families come from, we all have our favorite dishes. Comfort food speaks to feelings and flavors, aromas and memories, whether it's Sunday pot roast with creamy mashed potatoes, your Italian grandmother's spaghetti and meatballs, or classic New England baked beans. All these recipes have three things in common: They warm your heart, stir your soul, and happily fill your stomach.

In the Kitchen with David offers 150 hearty, easy, and comforting recipes. The portions are generous; the options are limitless. Recipes include quick Monday-to-Friday dinners as well as let-it-cook-all-day weekend suppers. If you're hosting a cocktail party with great appetizers, a big game-day party, or contributing a dish to a family reunion, you'll find everything you need. Foodie favorites, recipes that you voted for as

your best-loved dishes from the show, are scattered throughout the book. Look for the "Foodie Favorite" icon next to them. I've also added "Dishin' with David" tidbits that will streamline your cooking and save you time, and "Make It Your Own" suggestions that provide variations and substitutions.

My cookbook *In the Kitchen with David* is a dream come true for me. Every step of the process—deciding which recipes to include, testing, tasting, and writing about them—has been so exciting and given me the chance to further share my passion for classic comfort food. My heart and my tummy are both full as I send this book into your kitchen. My wish is that these recipes encourage you and your family to gather around the dinner table for great meals and, more important, great memories.

KEEP IT FLAVORFUL!

David

appetizers
═══ party starters! ═══

COOKING AND ENTERTAINING go hand in hand for me. I love doing both! No matter the occasion, gatherings at my home always start with some fantastic appetizers. Delicious dips, piping-hot poppers, and crispy potato skins are just some of the starters I've included in this chapter. All are easy. All are tasty. And all are sure to keep your guests coming back for more.

I usually figure on four or five appetizers per person with before-dinner cocktails. Give your guests just enough small bites to tempt their appetites, but also leave room for the rest of the meal you've prepared. If I'm throwing an appetizers-and-drinks-only party, then I double the amount of appetizers.

The secret to throwing memorable parties? Organization. That means planning ahead. Way ahead. Creatively balance your menu with made-the-day-before dips and hot appetizers. Do as much prepping and cooking ahead of time as you can. You don't want to spend the entire party pulling trays of Cheddar-Ham Cups, Skewered Buffalo Chicken Tenders, and Chicken Nachos from the oven while everyone else is laughing it up in the living room. Dips taste best when made in advance so the flavors have time to develop. Fill and fry the Cheeseburger Dumplings a day or two ahead, then pop them in the oven when the first guests ring your doorbell. Then get the party started!

guacamole cups
with pico de gallo

When you're hosting a party, it's fun to make dishes that are "out of the box." This recipe is one of those—and it's right out of a muffin pan. Your guests will think you spent hours making these cups, but actually, the process is simple. Just press egg roll wrappers (look for them in the produce section of your grocery store) into a mini muffin pan and bake. The filling for these cups is a classic, garlicky guacamole topped with a bit of pico de gallo—a fresh salsa. Some folks like a smooth guacamole, others chunky. I like the best of both worlds—smooth with a little chunkiness. Concerned about the heat? Cut back on the jalapeño.

MAKES 36 CUPS

Vegetable oil spray
1 pound package egg roll wrappers
4 ripe avocados
Juice of 1 lime
¾ cup jarred pico de gallo
3 garlic cloves, minced

1 teaspoon extra virgin olive oil
1 teaspoon seeded and minced jalapeño
1 teaspoon kosher salt

1 cup (8 ounces) sour cream
Cilantro sprigs

Preheat the oven to 350°F. Spray mini muffin pans with the vegetable oil spray. If you have just one muffin pan, the cups will need to be made in batches.

Cut the egg roll wrappers into quarters. Place a square in each of 36 mini muffin cups, gently pressing the wrappers against the bottoms and sides. Bake for 6 to 8 minutes, until light golden brown. Remove the cups from the pan and cool on a wire rack.

Halve the avocados, remove the pits, and scoop out the flesh into a bowl. Sprinkle the avocados with the lime juice.

Add the pico de gallo, garlic, olive oil, jalapeño, and salt. Using a fork, mash the mixture to the desired smoothness or chunkiness. Fill each egg roll cup with a spoonful of the guacamole. Top each one with a bit of the sour cream and a sprig of cilantro before serving.

make it your own

Only your imagination limits what you can fill these little cups with

- smoked salmon and cream cheese
- goat cheese and chopped apples
- shrimp salad with a sprig of dill
- crumbled cooked sausage and shredded Cheddar
- blue cheese and chopped pecans
- sautéed mushrooms and bacon bits

BE FLEXIBLE!

When working with egg roll wrappers, wet a paper towel and cover the wrappers. Using a damp paper towel makes the wrappers more pliable and easier to handle.

foodie FAVORITE

white bean and sun-dried tomato dip

When you're asked to bring an appetizer to a party or a family gathering, wow them with this easy-to-put-together dip. Pops of color from sun-dried tomatoes and bright green herbs make this savory spread a winner, and guests will no doubt hit you up for the recipe.

MAKES 3 CUPS

1 15-ounce can cannellini beans, drained and rinsed
2 tablespoons fresh lemon juice
¼ cup extra virgin olive oil
2 garlic cloves
1 teaspoon onion powder
Pinch of cayenne

1 3- to 4-ounce jar sun-dried tomatoes packed in olive oil, drained and patted dry
½ teaspoon chopped fresh rosemary
¼ teaspoon kosher salt
¼ teaspoon freshly ground black pepper
1 teaspoon chopped fresh chives
Toasted pita chips

Put the beans, lemon juice, olive oil, garlic, onion powder, cayenne, sun-dried tomatoes, rosemary, salt, and black pepper in a food processor. Pulse until the mixture is smooth.

Put the dip in a serving bowl. Before serving, garnish with the chives and serve with a basket of toasted pita chips. The dip can be refrigerated up to one to two days.

artichoke-spinach dip
in a bread bowl

While you'll find this popular appetizer in many restaurants, you'll be surprised how easy it is to make at home. The hardest part is hollowing out the bread and not eating all the pieces!

MAKES 4 CUPS

1 8-ounce package cream cheese, at room temperature
¼ cup mayonnaise
¼ cup (1 ounce) freshly grated Parmigiano-Reggiano
¼ cup (1 ounce) freshly grated Pecorino Romano
1 garlic clove, minced
½ teaspoon dried basil
¼ teaspoon garlic salt

Kosher salt and freshly ground black pepper to taste
1 14-ounce can artichoke hearts, drained and chopped
1 10-ounce package chopped frozen spinach, thawed, drained, and squeezed dry
⅓ cup (2½ ounces) shredded mozzarella
Bread bowl (see below) or pita chips

Preheat the oven to 350°F. Lightly grease a 1-quart ovenproof baking dish.

Mix together the cream cheese, mayonnaise, Parmigiano-Reggiano, pecorino, garlic, basil, garlic salt, kosher salt, and pepper in a medium bowl. Gently stir in the artichoke hearts and spinach. Transfer the mixture to the prepared baking dish. Sprinkle the mozzarella on top.

Bake for 25 minutes, until bubbly and lightly browned on top. Transfer the dip to a bread bowl (if using) or serve warm with pita chips or small toast.

dishin' *with* DAVID

THINK OUTSIDE THE BOWL

Hot soups, chunky stews, and fresh dips are always welcomed with big smiles and big appetites. But, when you add a bread bowl, you've just served the perfect comfort-food dish. Bread bowls are simply hollowed-out loaves of crusty round French or sourdough bread. And best of all, they're edible! Use larger loaves for dips and spreads; individual loaves for soups and stews.

Here's how to prepare them: Use a serrated knife to slice off the top of the round loaf. Pull out most of the soft interior, leaving a 1-inch thickness on the inside. Cut the bread into cubes and lightly toast to serve with the dip. Place the bread bowl on a serving plate and spoon the dip into the bowl. When serving soups and stews in bread bowls, use the top rounds as "lids." When guests remove their lids, they're greeted with the delicious aroma of your home-cooked creation. At this point, everyone's smiling around the table, and that's even before the first bite.

cheesy pepperoni dip
with pizza dippers

One of my favorite foods on the planet is pizza. I love it hot. I love it cold. Thin or thick crust. In any form or fashion. In true foodie tradition, I also love being creative with pizza. This recipe includes everything I want in my pie—in the form of a mouthwatering dip. It's cheesy, it's flavorful, and it's fun.

MAKES 32 DIPPERS

PIZZA CRUST DIPPERS

⅔ cup (about 2 ounces) freshly grated Parmigiano-Reggiano

1 teaspoon Italian seasoning

½ teaspoon garlic powder

2 13.8-ounce cans refrigerated pizza dough

½ cup extra virgin olive oil

CHEESY PEPPERONI DIP

12 ounces cream cheese, at room temperature

½ cup (4 ounces) sour cream

2 teaspoons dried oregano

1 teaspoon dried basil

¼ teaspoon red pepper flakes

1 garlic clove, minced

¾ cup prepared pizza or tomato sauce

1⅓ cup chopped pepperoni

½ cup chopped green bell pepper

¼ cup sliced scallions

¾ cup (3 ounces) shredded Cheddar

¾ cup (3 ounces) plus ¼ cup (1 ounce) shredded mozzarella

Preheat the oven to 425°F.

To make the dippers, combine the Parmigiano-Reggiano, Italian seasoning, and garlic powder in a bowl. Set aside. Roll out one pizza dough on a lightly floured work surface and cut into 18 squares. Then cut each square in half diagonally to form 2 triangles. Arrange the triangles on a baking sheet and brush each one with olive oil. Sprinkle the Parmesan mixture over the triangles. Repeat with the remaining pizza dough. There will be a total of 72 triangles. Bake for 10 to 12 minutes, until golden brown. Remove to a wire rack to cool.

To make the dip, whisk together the cream cheese, sour cream, oregano, basil, red pepper flakes, garlic, pizza sauce, pepperoni, bell pepper, scallions, Cheddar, and ¾ cup of the mozzarella in a bowl. Evenly spread out the mixture in a shallow 2-quart ovenproof dish.

Bake for 15 minutes, until bubbly. Remove from the oven and sprinkle with the remaining ¼ cup mozzarella. Bake for 5 minutes more. Serve hot with the dippers.

chicken nachos

You know how I love to feed crowds. Well, one of my all-time favorite crowd-pleasers is a ginormous platter of my cheesy, zippy, crunchy nachos. While nachos are often made with ground beef, I like to mix things up every once in a while by using shredded chicken for a different flavor profile. Leftover chicken or a store-bought rotisserie chicken makes these nachos easy to prepare.

MAKES 6 TO 8 SERVINGS

2 teaspoons chili powder

2 teaspoons ground cumin

1 teaspoon garlic powder

1 teaspoon kosher salt

2 cups cooked and shredded chicken

1 13.5-ounce bag tortilla chips

2 poblano peppers, roasted (see below) and chopped

2 medium tomatoes, seeded and diced

1 15-ounce can black beans, rinsed and drained

1 8-ounce package shredded Mexican cheese blend

4 to 5 scallions, minced

¾ cup chopped fresh cilantro

Preheat the oven to 375°F.

Stir together the chili powder, cumin, garlic powder, and salt in a small bowl. Add the shredded chicken and toss evenly to coat.

Spread the tortilla chips in an even layer on a large baking sheet. Evenly top the chips with the chicken, followed by the chiles, tomatoes, and black beans. Finish with the cheese and scallions. Bake for 8 to 10 minutes, until the cheese is melted and bubbly and the nachos are heated through. Remove from the oven and top with the cilantro. Using a wide spatula, transfer the nachos to a serving plate.

Make it your own

Pass bowls filled with salsa, crumbled bacon, avocado slices, and sour cream to top off the nachos.

dishin' with DAVID

ROASTED PEPPERS

Roasting chiles or bell peppers mellows their intense flavors and makes it easy to remove the tough skins. Preheat the broiler. Line a baking sheet with aluminum foil. Place the chiles or bell peppers on the foil and roast for 6 to 8 minutes. Using tongs, turn the peppers so their skins blister and char evenly on all sides. When they are charred and blackened all over, remove the peppers to a bowl and cover with plastic wrap. The steam helps loosen the skins. When the peppers are cool enough to handle, use your fingers to peel off the skins. It's just fine if you can't remove all of those charred bits. Don't run them under water—you'll wash away all those flavorful juices. Once they are roasted and peeled, you can chop or slice the peppers as directed, or cover and refrigerate them for several days.

bacon, caramelized onions, and gorgonzola bruschetta

To me, bacon is the world's most perfect food. It's salty, it's smoky, it's crispy, and it's the absolute perfect comfort food (more on that in Pork: The Divine Swine, page 121). This appetizer combines bacon, slowly caramelized onions, and robust Gorgonzola and is served on tiny, toasty pieces of French baguette. Your party guests will find these bites hard to resist. Be sure to save a few for yourself.

MAKES 12 BRUSCHETTA

½ pound bacon slices, cut into 2-inch pieces

2 tablespoons unsalted butter

3 large onions, halved and thinly sliced

1 teaspoon kosher salt

1 tablespoon sugar

1 French baguette, sliced diagonally into twelve 1-inch pieces

1 large garlic clove, halved

1 teaspoon extra virgin olive oil

½ cup (2 ounces) crumbled Gorgonzola

Put the bacon slices in a cold skillet and cook over medium heat for 3 to 4 minutes on each side, turning just once, until desired crispness. Transfer the bacon to paper towels to drain. Discard all but 1 tablespoon of the bacon drippings from the skillet.

Add the butter and onions to the skillet with the bacon drippings. Cook over low heat, stirring occasionally. After 10 minutes, sprinkle the salt and sugar over the onions to help caramelize them. Cook for 12 to 15 minutes more, until the onions turn a rich caramel color. Don't let them burn. Set aside.

Adjust an oven rack to just below the broiler. Set the oven to broil.

Rub both sides of the bread slices with the garlic. Using a pastry brush, lightly brush one side of each slice with olive oil. Place the slices, oil side down, on a baking sheet. Toast the bread for 3 to 4 minutes, until the bread just begins to brown. Using tongs, remove the bread slices to a wire rack to cool, but don't turn off the oven.

Top each oiled side of the bread slices with some of the bacon and onions. Sprinkle the Gorgonzola on top. Return the bruschetta to the oven for 1 minute, or until the cheese has melted. Serve immediately.

dishin' *with*
DAVID

WEIGHTS AND MEASURES AND CHEESE

You'll notice in the ingredients that I've listed the equivalent of 8 ounces of cheese—Cheddar or Monterey Jack—as 2 cups. You must be thinking, "I know that eight ounces equals one cup. What on earth is David talking about?" Well, shredded or grated cheese is sold by weight, not volume. So, if you're buying shredded cheese or grating your own, know that 8 ounces in weight equals 2 cups in volume. Here's a handy chart to make your shopping easier:

WEIGHT	VOLUME
1 pound cheese (16 ounces)	4 cups shredded
8 ounces	2 cups shredded
4 ounces	1 cup shredded
3 ounces	¾ cup shredded
2 ounces	½ cup shredded
1 ounce	¼ cup shredded

cheddar-broccoli poppers
with ranch dipping sauce

You're going to love these piping-hot, fresh-from-the-fryer poppers. As soon as you bite into their crispy, golden brown crust, you'll taste the gooey cheese. Then…wait for it…there's the bite of the broccoli. Just when you think they can't get any better, dip one into the creamy ranch sauce. You'd better make a double batch; one won't be enough for your hungry guests.

MAKES 20 TO 24 POPPERS

1 16-ounce package frozen chopped broccoli

3 cups (12 ounces) shredded sharp Cheddar

3 plus 2 large eggs, lightly beaten

1 teaspoon kosher salt

½ teaspoon freshly ground black pepper

½ teaspoon garlic powder

2 cups dry bread crumbs

Canola oil for frying

Kosher salt and freshly ground black pepper

1 cup bottled ranch dressing

Cook the broccoli according to package directions, about 5 minutes. Drain and dry the broccoli in a salad spinner or with paper towels to remove excess water. Chop finely. Broccoli should be warm when adding other ingredients.

Mix together the broccoli, Cheddar, the 3 beaten eggs, salt, pepper, and garlic powder in a large bowl. Using your hands, shape the mixture into 1-inch balls.

Put the bread crumbs on a shallow plate. Dip the balls into one of the bowls with the 2 beaten eggs, then roll them in the bread crumbs. Refrigerate the balls for 20 minutes. Dip the balls back into the bowl with the beaten eggs, then roll them again in the bread crumbs. Place the balls on a baking sheet and keep refrigerated until ready to fry.

Clip a deep-frying thermometer to the side of a heavy, deep pot. Add 3 inches of canola oil to the pot and slowly heat to 375°F. Using a slotted spoon, add 6 poppers to the hot oil and fry until golden brown on one side, 1 to 2 minutes. Turn them and fry for 1 or 2 minutes more. (Cook the poppers in batches or the oil won't stay hot and the poppers will be soggy rather than crisp.) Using tongs, remove the fried poppers to a wire rack or paper towels. Season with salt and pepper. Cook the remaining poppers. Serve hot with the ranch dressing.

st. louis fried ravioli
with marinara sauce

If you want a great cheese steak, go to Philadelphia. If you want a great po'boy, go to New Orleans. And if you want great fried ravioli, go to St. Louis. What? It's true. Locals call these perfect bites toasted ravioli rather than fried, but you'd be hard pressed to find a restaurant in St. Louis that doesn't have these tasty little nuggets on the menu. Legend has it they were created when a chef mistakenly dropped a batch of ravioli into a pot of oil rather than boiling water. No matter how these came to be, enjoy them right away with some zesty marinara sauce.

MAKES 24 RAVIOLI

3 large eggs

2 cups all-purpose flour

2 cups Italian-style bread crumbs

24 small fresh ravioli, such as Buitoni

Canola oil for frying

½ teaspoon kosher salt

½ teaspoon coarsely ground black pepper

¼ cup (1 ounce) freshly grated
   Parmigiano-Reggiano

2 cups Marinara Sauce (page 198)

Put the eggs, flour, and bread crumbs in three separate shallow bowls. Beat the eggs. Working in batches, dip each ravioli in the egg to coat completely. Allow the excess egg to drip back into the bowl. Dredge the ravioli in the flour and then in the bread crumbs. Place the ravioli on a large plate and continue with the remaining ravioli.

Clip a deep-frying thermometer to the side of a heavy, deep pot. Add 3 inches canola oil to the pot and slowly heat the oil to 325°F. Using a slotted spoon, add 4 or 5 ravioli to the hot oil and fry until golden brown, about 3 minutes, turning them halfway through cooking. (Cook the ravioli in batches or the oil won't stay hot and they will be soggy rather than crisp.) Using tongs, remove the fried ravioli to a wire rack or paper towels. Cook the remaining ravioli. Sprinkle the hot ravioli with the salt, pepper, and Parmigiano-Reggiano. Serve hot, accompanied by a bowl of warm marinara sauce for dipping.

dishin' with DAVID

GET YOUR DEGREE IN FRYING

A deep-frying thermometer clipped to the side of the pot is the most accurate way to tell if the cooking oil is hot enough. The ideal oil temperature is 350°F to 365°F for frying. If you don't have a thermometer, stick the end of a wooden spoon into the heated oil. If bubbles form around the wood and float toward the surface, the oil is hot enough for frying.

crispy potato skins

You know, I've never met a potato I didn't like. But when the skin of a potato is baked until it's crispy, crunchy, and toasty and then filled with two of my favorite ingredients—cheese and bacon—it can rival a bowl of mashed potatoes any day. Add the cheese, don't skimp on the bacon, and don't forget that fresh rosemary. As soon as you taste the first bite, you'll be saying, "Mashed what?"

MAKES 8 SERVINGS

4 medium baking potatoes
¼ cup extra virgin olive oil
1 tablespoon minced fresh rosemary
Freshly ground black pepper

½ pound bacon slices, cooked (page 137) and crumbled
2 cups (8 ounces) shredded Cheddar
½ teaspoon kosher salt
1 cup (8 ounces) sour cream

Preheat the oven to 375°F.

Scrub the potatoes with a vegetable brush and pierce each one several times with a fork. Bake until the skins are crisp and a knife goes easily through the flesh, 50 minutes to 1 hour. Remove the potatoes from the oven. Leave the oven on.

Because the potatoes will be very hot, use a towel or oven mitt to protect your hands. Cut the potatoes in half lengthwise and scoop out the flesh, leaving about ⅛ inch of the potato flesh attached to the skin. (Don't discard all that good potato; mash the pulp with a little butter and milk until smooth and save for another use.)

Brush the inside of each potato skin with some olive oil. Sprinkle on the rosemary and a few grinds of pepper. Top each one with some crumbled bacon, Cheddar, and salt. Arrange the skins on a baking sheet and bake for 5 to 10 minutes until crisp. Serve immediately with the sour cream on the side.

cheddar-ham cups

When I host brunch at my house, I like to greet my hungry friends and family with big platters of these bite-size bits of comfort. Bursting with lots of ham, cheese, and bacon, these savory starters keep everyone satisfied until we sit down for the main event.

MAKES 32 CUPS

Vegetable oil spray
2 cups (8 ounces) finely shredded
    Cheddar
½ cup thinly sliced, finely chopped
    smoked ham
¾ cup mayonnaise
½ cup finely chopped onion

4 to 5 bacon slices, cooked (page 137)
    and finely crumbled
2 to 3 teaspoons Dijon mustard
¼ teaspoon kosher salt
1 16.3-ounce tube (8 biscuits) Pillsbury
    Grands! Flaky Layers
Freshly ground black pepper

Preheat the oven to 450°F. Spray a mini muffin pan with the vegetable oil spray, even if using a nonstick pan.

Toss together the Cheddar, ham, mayonnaise, onion, bacon, mustard, and salt in a medium bowl.

Gently separate the individual biscuits. Cut each biscuit into quarters. Roll each biscuit quarter into a 1-inch ball and press the dough into the bottom and up the sides of the muffin cups. Fill each cup with ½ teaspoon of the cheese-ham mixture. Take care not to overfill them. Sprinkle a grind of pepper on top of each one.

Bake for 5 to 7 minutes, until golden brown and the cheese is melted. Let stand for 2 minutes before removing from the pan. Serve warm.

cheesy crab-stuffed mushrooms

Crab-stuffed mushrooms may have you thinking about fancy five-star restaurants. But fancy food doesn't have to be, and often isn't, difficult to prepare, as this recipe proves. You can make this dish easily at home—even ahead of time. Cover, refrigerate, and pop the mushrooms into the oven as your first guest arrives. Everyone will be so impressed.

MAKES 12 TO 16 MUSHROOMS

1 pound (12 to 16) mushrooms, 1 to 1½ inches in diameter
2 tablespoons unsalted butter
2 tablespoons chopped onion
½ cup fresh, soft bread cubes
½ cup (4 ounces) fresh crabmeat, picked over and finely chopped

½ teaspoon kosher salt
2 teaspoons fresh lemon juice
½ teaspoon Worcestershire sauce
2 tablespoons chopped fresh parsley
½ cup dry white wine
½ cup (2 ounces) shredded Cheddar

Preheat the oven to 400°F.

Remove the stems from the mushrooms and set aside the caps. Finely chop the stems.

Melt the butter in a small skillet over medium heat. Add the onion and stems and sauté for 4 to 5 minutes. Add the bread cubes and crabmeat, stirring constantly until lightly brown. Stir in the salt, lemon juice, Worcestershire sauce, and parsley.

Fill the mushroom caps with the crab mixture. Arrange the mushrooms in a single layer in a shallow baking dish. Pour the white wine in the bottom of the baking dish. Bake for 15 minutes. Remove the dish from the oven and sprinkle on the Cheddar. Bake for 8 to 10 minutes more, until the cheese melts. Serve hot.

dishin' with DAVID

A WORLD OF INGREDIENTS, BUT NOT A WORLD AWAY

I asked one of the Two Hot Tamales, chef Susan Feniger, where people can find Mexican spices and ingredients, and she told me, "Now, it's really pretty easy to find great Latin ingredients. For sure, online you can find almost anything. But in every major grocery store across the country you can find Mexican cheeses, dried chiles like chipotles and anchos, and tamarind. And really, even without all those special ingredients, you can still make great Latin food because every store has cumin, cayenne, and other spices. Just do a little research to understand the ingredients."

That's so true, not just for Mexican foods, but for Southeast Asian, Indian, Middle Eastern, and other cuisines.

tex-mex chicken roll ups

Inspired by the food I had while visiting the QVC facility in San Antonio, Texas, this will have everyone at your next party saying, *"Muy bueno!"* Visit any restaurant along the city's famous River Walk and you'll find the best of both worlds: Tex-Mex cuisine. These bites are my own special combination of chicken, peppers, cheese, and spices all wrapped up in flour tortillas, baked, and then sliced.

MAKES 10 SERVINGS

Vegetable oil spray

2 tablespoons extra virgin olive oil

2 small onions, chopped

¼ red bell pepper, cored, seeded, and diced

1 jalapeño, stemmed, seeded, and diced

2 garlic cloves, chopped

4 large button mushrooms, sliced

¾ cup prepared taco sauce

3 cups cooked and shredded chicken

2 cups (8 ounces) grated Monterey Jack

1 teaspoon kosher salt

1 teaspoon cayenne

10 8-inch flour tortillas

Guacamole (page 4) or salsa

Preheat the oven to 350°F. Spray a 9 x 13-inch shallow baking dish with the vegetable oil spray.

Heat the olive oil in a skillet over medium heat. Add the onions, bell pepper, jalapeño, garlic, and mushrooms and cook for 1 minute. Stir in the taco sauce and cook until heated through, 1 to 2 minutes. Add the chicken, salt, and cayenne and toss to coat. Add the Monterey Jack. Cover and simmer for 5 minutes.

Place a tortilla on a clean work surface. Spoon 2 tablespoons of the chicken mixture on top and spread it to the tortilla's edges. Roll up and place in the prepared baking dish. Continue with the rest of the tortillas, putting the filled and rolled ones next to one another. Bake for 10 minutes, until hot and the cheese is melted.

Remove each tortilla from the baking dish to a cutting board and slice diagonally into 6 pieces. Arrange the slices on a serving platter, accompanied by a bowl of guacamole or salsa.

cheeseburger dumplings
with steak sauce

Here's a melding of two culinary classics combined into one East-meets-West duo—true-blue all-American cheeseburger used as a filling for Asian dumplings, all served with a zesty home-made steak dipping sauce. And there's certainly no confusion about that! I'm not one for playing favorites, but these are some of the tastiest little treats I've ever had.

MAKES 48 DUMPLINGS

CHEESEBURGER FILLING

1 pound ground beef

1 cup finely chopped gherkins or pickle relish, drained

1 small onion, finely chopped

2 teaspoons Worcestershire sauce

2 heaping teaspoons Dijon mustard

1 teaspoon kosher salt

½ teaspoon freshly ground black pepper

STEAK SAUCE

1 cup ketchup

3 tablespoons Dijon mustard

1 tablespoon red wine vinegar

1 tablespoon molasses

2 tablespoons Worcestershire sauce

DUMPLINGS

2 large eggs

2 packages (24 each) round pot sticker or gyoza wrappers

20 slices American cheese, quartered and cut into ½-inch strips

¼ cup canola oil

Preheat the oven to 350°F.

To make the filling, combine the ground beef, gherkins, onion, Worcestershire sauce, mustard, salt, and pepper in a large bowl. Mix well by hand or with a spoon and season with the salt and pepper. Cover and refrigerate for at least 30 minutes.

To make the sauce, whisk together the ketchup, mustard, vinegar, molasses, and Worcestershire sauce in a small bowl until smooth. Cover and set aside while preparing the dumplings.

To make the dumplings, make an egg wash, lightly beating the eggs with 2 teaspoons water in a small bowl. Set aside.

Spoon 1 teaspoon filling on one side of a circular wrapper. Top with a strip of cheese. (Cover the other wrappers with a damp paper towel to keep them from drying out.) Using a pastry brush, brush the edges of each dumpling with the egg wash. Fold the unfilled side over to create a half moon. Press to seal the edges. Place the filled dumpling on a baking sheet. Continue until all the wrappers and filling are used.

Heat the canola oil in a large skillet over medium-high heat until it's almost smoking. Using a spatula, gently transfer 4 or 5 dumplings to the skillet and cook for 2 to 3 minutes. Turn them over and cook until lightly browned, 2 to 3 minutes more. Transfer the dumplings to the baking sheet and bake them for 5 minutes. Serve warm with the steak sauce.

skewered buffalo chicken tenders
with blue cheese sauce

Let's take a trip to Buffalo, New York, home of those spicy-hot chicken wings. Here, the same great flavors we all know and love come in my version of these no-mess, no-fuss, easy-to-serve appetizers. First, they're made with boneless chicken tenders. And second, they offer that great spicy, blue cheesy flavor—all handed to your guests on a skewer. It's great party food done with absolute ease. You can use either metal or bamboo skewers. If using bamboo skewers, be sure to soak them in water for 15 minutes before putting the chicken on them so they don't go up in smoke.

MAKES 8 TO 10 SERVINGS

Vegetable oil spray

CHICKEN SKEWERS

½ cup all-purpose flour
½ cup plain bread crumbs
Pinch of garlic powder
Pinch of paprika
½ teaspoon kosher salt

½ teaspoon coarsely ground black pepper
2 large eggs, lightly beaten
1 pound chicken tenders or 4 boneless, skinless chicken breasts, cut into ½-inch strips

BUFFALO HOT SAUCE

¾ cup hot sauce
5 tablespoons unsalted butter

1 teaspoon minced garlic

1 to 2 cups bottled blue cheese dressing
3 celery stalks, cut into 3-inch pieces

Preheat the oven to 350°F. Line a baking sheet with aluminum foil and spray with the vegetable oil spray.

To make the chicken skewers, combine the flour, bread crumbs, garlic powder, paprika, salt, and pepper in a resealable plastic bag. Close the bag and shake thoroughly. Place the beaten eggs in a shallow bowl. Dip the chicken tenders into the egg, shaking off any extra. Put the chicken tenders into the flour mixture, close the bag, and shake thoroughly to coat.

Thread the chicken onto the skewers. Arrange the skewers in a single layer on the prepared baking sheet. Bake for 7 to 8 minutes, then turn the skewers over and bake for 7 to 8 minutes more.

To make the sauce, while the chicken is cooking, combine the hot sauce, butter, and garlic in a saucepan over medium heat. Stir well.

Remove the baking sheet from the oven. Brush both sides of the chicken with the Buffalo Hot Sauce. Return the chicken to the oven and bake for 3 minutes more. Serve with the blue cheese dressing and celery sticks.

teriyaki chicken wings

I'm always looking for new ways to prepare wings. You can purchase teriyaki sauce or make your own by whisking together soy sauce, mirin (Japanese rice wine), and a touch of brown sugar. This teriyaki sauce on chicken wings is a nice changeup from Buffalo-style or barbecued ones. Why not give it a try?

MAKES 10 TO 12 WINGS

Vegetable oil spray

TERIYAKI SAUCE

1 cup chopped fresh pineapple or
    1 8-ounce can crushed pineapple

½ cup low-sodium soy sauce

¼ cup mirin or dry sherry

Juice of 1 lime

Juice of ½ orange

1 tablespoon rice vinegar or apple cider
    vinegar

1 teaspoon toasted sesame oil

¼ cup packed dark brown sugar

1 2-inch piece fresh ginger, peeled and
    minced

2 garlic cloves

2 tablespoons cornstarch

¼ teaspoon red pepper flakes

CHICKEN WINGS

1½ pounds chicken wings

1 scallion, minced

Preheat the oven to 425°F. Spray a 9 x 13-inch baking dish with the vegetable oil spray.

To make the sauce, combine the pineapple, soy sauce, mirin, lime juice, orange juice, rice vinegar, sesame oil, brown sugar, ginger, and garlic in a blender and blend until smooth. For a smoother sauce, strain the mixture through a fine-mesh sieve.

Whisk the cornstarch with 1½ tablespoons cold water in a small bowl until smooth. Pour the teriyaki sauce into a medium saucepan, add the red pepper flakes, and bring to a boil over medium heat. Remove the sauce from the heat and immediately stir in the cornstarch mixture. Stir constantly until the sauce thickens. Allow the sauce to cool.

Place the chicken wings in the prepared dish and pour the sauce over them. Bake, uncovered, until the wings are golden brown, about 45 minutes. Remove to a platter and garnish with the scallion before serving.

biscuits, muffins, _and_ quick breads
═══ our daily bread ═══

HAVE YOU EVER walked by a bakery and suddenly the warm, comforting aroma of butter, sugar, and flour baking together whisks you back to your childhood? Those moments remind me of all the delicious baked goodness that came out of my mother's and my grandmothers' kitchens. When I want to re-create those memories in my own kitchen, I whip up some homemade biscuits, muffins, or quick breads.

Besides some of the delicious treats I grew up with, this chapter also features some recent additions to my lineup. I call these my "makin', bakin', and takin'" recipes. Make and bake a basket of Cheddar-Bacon Biscuits, a muffin tin with Banana–Peanut Butter Muffins, or a loaf of Pumpkin Bread with Cream Cheese Frosting to take as gifts to any gathering. There's something so lovely and inviting about these recipes; they make everyone feel like they're back home again.

southern buttermilk biscuits

Both of my grandmothers had a knack for making hot-out-of-the-oven, light and flaky biscuits that would almost float off the countertop all by themselves.

Slather with sweet butter and drizzle with some honey. Or even better, take a fork (yes, a fork) and pull a biscuit apart. Tuck a slice of salty country ham between the halves. I could eat a whole batch of these flaky biscuits in one sitting. I'll try to control myself and save one or two for you.

MAKES 6 TO 8 BISCUITS

4 cups all-purpose flour

2 tablespoons baking powder

2 tablespoons sugar

2 teaspoons kosher salt

⅔ cup butter-flavor all-vegetable

shortening, chilled and cut into ½-inch dice

2 cups buttermilk

2 tablespoons unsalted butter, melted

Preheat the oven to 450°F.

Combine the flour, baking powder, sugar, and salt in a large bowl and whisk to blend. Add the shortening. Using a pastry cutter or two knives, cut through the shortening and flour until the mixture resembles coarse meal. Add the buttermilk and mix just until combined. The dough will be very moist and sticky.

Turn the dough out onto a well-floured board or work surface and gently pat or roll it into a round about ½ inch thick. Fold the dough into thirds, as if folding a letter, and reroll it into a round 2 inches thick.

Using a 3-inch biscuit cutter, cut the dough into rounds. Gather up the scraps, gently roll out the dough, and cut out additional biscuits. Transfer the biscuits to a nonstick baking sheet. Bake the biscuits for 10 to 12 minutes, until they are puffed and golden brown. Let cool on a wire rack until you can't wait any longer. As the biscuits cool, brush the tops with the melted butter.

dishin' with DAVID

BISCUIT LOVERS

There are as many biscuit recipes as there are biscuit lovers. To make your biscuits stand out from all the rest, follow these easy tips: Make sure the buttermilk and the shortening are ice cold. And if you want fluffy, flaky biscuits, don't overmix, overhandle, or overknead the dough. A gentle touch means light and airy biscuits.

mom's mayonnaise drop biscuits

Mayonnaise biscuits? Yup, you read that correctly. My mother has made these biscuits for as long as I can remember. They have an incredible, tangy, sourdough flavor from a touch of apple cider vinegar, and a denser texture than buttermilk biscuits. They're also unique because mayonnaise takes the place of cold shortening or butter. Self-rising flour cuts out having to measure baking powder and salt. And the batter is dropped into muffin cups, so you don't have to use a biscuit cutter. Mom always served these biscuits to sop up the gravy from pot roast, chicken, or pork chops, so make sure you have plenty of biscuits on hand.

MAKES 12 BISCUITS

Vegetable oil spray

1 cup plus 2 tablespoons whole milk

3 tablespoons distilled white vinegar

2 cups self-rising flour

⅓ cup mayonnaise (not light or reduced fat)

Preheat the oven to 450°F. Generously spray a 12-cup muffin pan with the vegetable oil spray.

Combine the milk and vinegar in a measuring cup and stir to blend. Combine the flour and mayonnaise in a large bowl and stir until combined. The batter will be stiff. Add the milk-vinegar mixture and stir with a fork until just combined. Don't overmix. Evenly divide the batter among the cups of the prepared muffin pan.

Bake the biscuits for 15 minutes, until puffy and golden brown. Serve immediately.

dishin' with DAVID

SELF-RISING FLOUR

If you don't have self-rising flour in your pantry, don't worry. For each cup called for in a recipe, mix together 1 cup all-purpose flour, 1 teaspoon baking powder, and ¼ teaspoon kosher salt. If there's any other baking powder or salt in the recipe, omit it.

cheddar-bacon biscuits

There are times when buttermilk biscuits are just what you want, but there are other moments when you need something that packs a bit more of a punch—like these biscuits made with Cheddar cheese and bacon—two of the most delicious ingredients on earth. They're perfect as a side dish, but be careful, you might just end up making a meal out of the whole batch. If I want to make a breakfast sandwich, all I have to do is put a scoop of scrambled eggs between two halves and I'm good to go.

MAKES 8 TO 10 LARGE BISCUITS

2 cups all-purpose flour

2 teaspoons baking powder

2 teaspoons sugar

¾ teaspoon baking soda

½ teaspoon kosher salt

5 tablespoons unsalted butter, chilled and cut into ½-inch dice

1 garlic clove, minced

1½ cups (6 ounces) grated Cheddar

5 bacon slices, cooked (page 137) and crumbled

1 cup buttermilk

Preheat the oven to 425°F. Line a baking sheet with parchment paper.

Whisk together the flour, baking powder, sugar, baking soda, and salt in a large bowl. Add the butter. Using a pastry cutter or fork, gently work the butter into the dry ingredients until the mixture resembles a coarse meal. Stir in the garlic, Cheddar, and bacon. Add the buttermilk and stir just until the mixture comes together. The dough should be shaggy and moist.

Gather the dough into a ball and transfer it to a lightly floured work surface. Knead it gently a few times, and pat or roll it into a disk about ½ inch thick. Fold the dough 3 times, as if folding a letter, and roll out into a rectangle approximately 9 x 13 inches and about 1 inch thick.

Using a 4-inch biscuit cutter, cut the dough into rounds. Gather up the scraps, gently roll out the dough, and cut out additional biscuits. Transfer the biscuits to the prepared baking sheet. Bake for 12 to 15 minutes, until the biscuits are puffed and light golden brown. Serve warm.

skillet corn bread

with scallions and cheddar

When I was a little boy, we had dinner at my grandmother Mimi's once a week. While she changed the menu from meal to meal, one thing was always on the table: savory corn bread that was baked and served in a seasoned cast-iron skillet that she had owned for decades. There truly is a difference between corn bread made in a cast-iron skillet or in a regular baking dish. A properly cared for cast-iron skillet that's been repeatedly oiled and wiped, never washed out, just gets better and better the more you use it.

MAKES 8 TO 10 SERVINGS

2 tablespoons canola oil
¾ cup all-purpose flour
¾ cup yellow cornmeal
1 tablespoon sugar
1 teaspoon kosher salt
2 teaspoons baking powder
1 teaspoon baking soda

4 tablespoons (½ stick) unsalted butter, melted
1 large egg
1¼ cups buttermilk
½ cup chopped scallions (white and light green parts)
½ cup (2 ounces) shredded sharp Cheddar

Preheat the oven to 400°F.

Pour the canola oil into a 10-inch cast-iron skillet. Put the skillet in the oven for 10 minutes to preheat while you prepare the batter.

Combine the flour, cornmeal, sugar, salt, baking powder, and baking soda in a large bowl and whisk to blend. In a small bowl, combine the melted butter, egg, and buttermilk and whisk to blend. Pour the egg mixture into the flour mixture all at once. Add the scallions and Cheddar. Using a spatula or large wooden spoon, gently fold the ingredients together until they are just incorporated, about twelve folds. It's okay if there are still a few streaks of flour or cornmeal.

dishin' with DAVID

NO BUTTERMILK? NO PROBLEM!

You've got a pot of my Ultimate Game-Day Chili (page 147) simmering on the stove top for supper. Time to make the skillet corn bread, but you realize that there's no buttermilk in the fridge. Here's a foodie favorite tip: Just add a tablespoon of distilled white vinegar to whole milk and let it sit for a minute or two until you see it curdling. Ta-da! You've got buttermilk.

Using an oven mitt, remove the hot skillet from the oven. Pour in the batter and return the skillet to the oven. Bake for 10 minutes, then check the corn bread and rotate the skillet back to front so that it browns evenly. Continue to bake the corn bread until it is golden brown, about 10 minutes more.

Using oven mitts, remove the skillet from the oven and let the corn bread cool for 8 to 10 minutes. Place a plate facedown over the surface of the skillet and invert the skillet so that the corn bread falls onto the plate. Slice the corn bread into wedges and serve.

dishin' with
DAVID

SOME SALTY TALK

There are three types of salt you'll find on grocery store shelves, and here are the differences among them:

- Table salt is what you find in most homes and restaurants. To make the salt free-flowing, an anticaking agent and other additives like iodine are added and give table salt a chemical taste that many cooks try to avoid.
- Kosher salt is refined like table salt, but it doesn't have any additives. Kosher salt is available in coarse or fine grains, the latter being best for baking.
- Sea salt is literally seawater that has evaporated. Since the method is so time-consuming, pure sea salt is more expensive than table or kosher salt, but it also tastes so much better. Look for sea salts from Hawaii, France, and England, especially.

I prefer kosher salt for most of my cooking and baking and use a sprinkle of sea salt to finish off dishes like grilled steak or chicken, fresh salads, and cooked vegetables.

make it your own

Add to the batter
- ½ cup cooked and chopped crispy bacon
- ½ cup frozen corn kernels, thawed
- ½ cup chopped ham
- ½ cup minced red or green bell pepper
- 1 4-ounce can chopped green chiles, drained
- ¼ to ½ teaspoon cayenne
- Monterey Jack, with or without chiles, herbs, or vegetables, for the Cheddar

FLOUR POWER

I like my muffins with some blueberries in every bite. Not just on the bottom. To keep your blueberries from heading south, lightly dust them with 2 or 3 tablespoons of flour before adding them to the batter. Use an ice cream scoop to measure out the batter in equal amounts. This guarantees that your muffins will bake evenly without a soggy one in the bunch.

blueberry muffins
with streusel topping

Any bread or muffin is always better when you add fresh fruit. When I was a little boy, I used to spread butter on piping-hot blueberry muffins and watched it pool and run all over those sweet breakfast treats. These muffins are soft, the blueberries are plump, and just a little lemon adds brightness. Be sure to make a full batch—you'll want to snack on these later in the day, long after breakfast is over.

MAKES 12 MUFFINS

STREUSEL TOPPING

6 tablespoons (¾ stick) unsalted butter, softened
¼ cup packed light brown sugar
¼ cup granulated sugar
⅔ cup all-purpose flour
1¼ teaspoons ground cinnamon

MUFFINS

1¼ cups all-purpose flour
1 teaspoon baking powder
¼ teaspoon baking soda
¼ teaspoon kosher salt
½ cup vegetable oil
1 cup sugar
2 large eggs, at room temperature
½ cup (4 ounces) sour cream
2 teaspoons pure vanilla extract
Finely grated zest of one lemon
3 cups (about 1½ pints) fresh blueberries, rinsed, dried, and tossed with 2 to 3 tablespoons all-purpose flour

Preheat the oven to 350°F. Line a standard 12-cup muffin pan with paper muffin cups.

To make the topping, cream the butter, brown sugar, and granulated sugar together in the bowl of an electric mixer until light and fluffy. Add the flour and cinnamon and mix until crumbly. Set aside.

To make the muffins, whisk together the flour, baking powder, baking soda, and salt in a medium bowl. Set aside.

Place the vegetable oil, sugar, eggs, sour cream, vanilla, and lemon zest in a bowl. Using a whisk, mix the wet ingredients until well combined. Pour the batter into the dry ingredients and mix until completely incorporated. Do not overmix. Using a spatula, fold the floured berries into the batter.

Divide the batter evenly among the muffin cups, filling each cup to the top. Sprinkle the streusel topping evenly over the muffins. Bake the muffins for 28 to 30 minutes, until a tester inserted into the center of a muffin comes out clean. Transfer the muffin pan to a wire rack and cool for 10 minutes. Turn the muffins out onto the wire rack and let cool for 5 minutes before serving.

make it your own

- Add ½ cup chopped walnuts.
- Substitute an equal amount of fresh or frozen raspberries or blackberries for the blueberries.
- Use orange instead of lemon zest.
- Add 1 teaspoon ground cinnamon, ¼ teaspoon ground ginger, and ¼ ground nutmeg to the dry ingredients.
- Replace ½ cup flour with an equal amount of cornmeal.

banana–peanut butter muffins

Anyone who knows me knows I go nuts for peanut butter. Creamy or chunky. It doesn't matter. If a dish or dessert includes peanut butter, I am the first one in line. This recipe was inspired by the peanut butter–banana sandwiches my mother made for me when I was a kid. There was nothing I loved more, especially when the peanut butter got stuck to the roof of my mouth. These are oh-so-easy to eat and are a welcome surprise in a lunch box or as an afternoon snack.

MAKES 12 MUFFINS

Vegetable oil spray

3 tablespoons sugar

MUFFINS

1½ cups all-purpose flour

1 teaspoon baking powder

1 teaspoon baking soda

½ teaspoon kosher salt

⅓ cup vegetable oil

¾ cup sugar

1 large egg, lightly beaten

1 teaspoon banana extract

4 ripe bananas, mashed

1 cup peanut butter chips

TOPPING

1 ripe banana sliced into 12 even slices

3 tablespoons sugar

Preheat the oven to 350°F. Coat a nonstick 12-cup muffin pan with the vegetable oil spray. Divide the 3 tablespoons of sugar equally among the bottoms of the muffin cups. Gently shake the pan to evenly coat the sides and bottoms of the cups with sugar.

To make the muffins, place the flour, baking powder, baking soda, and salt in a medium bowl. With a whisk lightly mix to evenly distribute the ingredients. Set aside.

Put the vegetable oil, sugar, egg, banana extract, and mashed bananas in the bowl of an electric mixer and, using the whisk attachment, mix the ingredients until completely combined. Add the dry ingredients and mix on low speed until all the ingredients are evenly incorporated. Using a spatula, fold in the peanut butter chips.

To prepare the topping, toss the banana slices with the sugar.

Divide the batter evenly among the muffin cups, filling each cup a little over three fourths of the way full. Top each muffin with a sugared slice of banana.

Bake the muffins for 22 to 26 minutes, until a tester inserted into the center of a muffin comes out clean. Transfer the muffin pan to a wire rack and cool for 8 minutes before turning out the muffins.

sour cream coffee cake

I love pairing a slice of this delicious cake with my morning cup of joe, although it's good at any time of the day. I raid the pantry of just about every ingredient to make this cake, which is flecked with cinnamon and walnuts. Adding sour cream to the batter makes the cake so moist that it melts in your mouth.

MAKES 16 SERVINGS

Vegetable oil spray

TOPPING

½ cup finely chopped walnuts

⅔ cup sugar

1 tablespoon plus 1 teaspoon ground cinnamon

CAKE

3 cups all-purpose flour

2 teaspoons baking powder

1 teaspoon baking soda

1 teaspoon kosher salt

½ pound (2 sticks) unsalted butter, at room temperature

2 cups sugar

4 large eggs

2 teaspoons pure vanilla extract

1¾ cups (14 ounces) sour cream

Preheat the oven to 350°F. Spray a 12-cup Bundt pan with the vegetable oil spray.

To make the topping, mix the walnuts, sugar, and cinnamon in a small bowl. Put 2 tablespoons of the topping in the prepared pan and toss to coat the pan. Set aside the remaining topping.

To make the coffee cake, whisk together the flour, baking powder, baking soda, and salt in a medium bowl. Set aside.

Combine the butter and sugar in the bowl of an electric mixer and beat until light and fluffy, about 5 minutes. Add the eggs, one at a time, beating on low speed after each addition. Add the vanilla. Gradually beat in the sour cream and the flour mixture, alternating the sour cream and flour mixture until combined. Stop the mixer to scrape down the sides of the bowl as necessary.

Spread one third of the batter into the prepared Bundt pan and sprinkle on one third of the remaining topping. Repeat 2 more times.

Bake the cake for 1 hour to 1 hour and 10 minutes, until a tester inserted into the center of the cake comes out clean. Let cool on a wire rack for 1 hour. Invert the cake onto a plate. Serve warm or at room temperature.

HEY THERE, PUMPKIN!

Notice that the ingredients list says to buy canned pumpkin puree, not pumpkin pie filling. Why? Pumpkin pie filling contains added sugar and spices, while pure pumpkin puree is just that: pure pumpkin.

pumpkin bread
with cream cheese frosting

With good-quality canned pumpkin available year-round, you don't have to wait until the autumn to dig into this delicious recipe. Sweet, filled with spices, and topped with a cream cheese frosting, slices of the bread can be served for breakfast, dessert, or even with a cup of afternoon tea. Like most quick breads, make it a day ahead to maximize the flavors. Margarine is used in the frosting because it has less flavor than butter, allowing the taste of the cream cheese to stand out.

MAKES 12 SERVINGS

Vegetable oil spray

PUMPKIN BREAD

1 15-ounce can pumpkin puree
4 large eggs
½ cup canola oil
½ cup applesauce
⅔ cup fresh orange juice
2 teaspoons pure vanilla extract
1 cup granulated sugar
1 cup packed light brown sugar

3½ cups all-purpose flour
2 teaspoons baking soda
1¼ teaspoons kosher salt
1½ teaspoons ground cinnamon
1 teaspoon ground nutmeg
½ teaspoon ground cloves
1½ teaspoons ground ginger

CREAM CHEESE FROSTING

3 8-ounce packages cream cheese, at room temperature
8 tablespoons (1 stick) margarine, at room temperature (do not use butter)

1½ teaspoons pure vanilla extract
1 tablespoon fresh lemon juice
1 1-pound box confectioners' sugar, sifted

Preheat the oven to 350°F. Spray a 9 x 13-inch baking pan with the vegetable oil spray.

To make the bread, whisk together the pumpkin puree, eggs, canola oil, applesauce, orange juice, vanilla, granulated sugar, and brown sugar in a large bowl until well blended. Set aside.

In another bowl, combine the flour, baking soda, salt, cinnamon, nutmeg, cloves, and ginger. Pour half of the dry ingredients into the pumpkin mixture and stir well to combine. Then pour in the rest of the dry ingredients, mixing until just blended. Pour the mixture into the prepared baking pan.

Bake for 45 for 55 minutes, until a toothpick inserted into the center of the bread comes out clean. Let cool on a wire rack before icing.

To make the frosting, put the cream cheese and margarine in the bowl of an electric mixer. Cream on medium-low speed until smooth and free of any lumps. Mix in the vanilla and lemon juice. Carefully add the confectioners' sugar and whip until light and fluffy. Spread the frosting on the bread and refrigerate until slicing and serving.

warm cinnamon pull-apart bread
with cream cheese dipping sauce

A homemade gift of food says, "Here's a thank-you from my kitchen and my heart." I love giving homemade gifts of food throughout the year, but especially at Christmastime. And especially this cinnamony pull-apart bread. Your mail carrier, neighbors, friends, and even Santa Claus will appreciate this truly one-of-a-kind present. Pull each piece apart and watch that gooey cinnamon filling drizzle down the bread. Before popping the bread into your mouth, dip it in the cream cheese sauce. Just make sure you have a cold glass of milk to wash it down.

MAKES 6 TO 8 SERVINGS

Vegetable oil spray

PULL-APART BREAD

4 tablespoons (½ stick) unsalted butter

2 1-pound loaves frozen bread dough, thawed and briefly kneaded together

1 cup sugar

2 teaspoons ground cinnamon

1 cup golden raisins

½ teaspoon ground nutmeg

CREAM CHEESE DIPPING SAUCE

4 ounces cream cheese, at room temperature

1 cup confectioners' sugar

4 tablespoons (½ stick) unsalted butter, at room temperature

½ teaspoon pure vanilla extract

Position a rack in the center of the oven. Preheat the oven to 350°F. Spray an 8-inch square baking pan with the vegetable oil spray.

To make the bread, melt the butter in a small saucepan over medium-low heat, swirling the pan occasionally, until the butter becomes golden brown and smells nutty, 3 to 4 minutes. Set aside to cool slightly.

On a lightly floured work surface, use a floured rolling pin to roll the bread dough out into a 9 x 13-inch rectangle. Using a pastry brush, evenly brush the browned butter on the dough. Combine the sugar, cinnamon, and nutmeg in a small bowl and sprinkle on top of the buttered dough. Evenly sprinkle the raisins over the cinnamon sugar.

Starting at the short end closest to you, roll the dough into a log. Cut the log crosswise into 2-inch-thick slices. Arrange the slices, cut side up, side by side in the prepared baking pan. Bake the bread for 30 to 35 minutes, until it is puffed and the top is a deep golden brown. Let the bread cool on a wire rack for 5 minutes and turn out onto a platter before serving.

To make the sauce, combine the cream cheese, confectioners' sugar, butter, and vanilla in the bowl of an electric mixer. Beat until creamy and smooth.

Serve the bread warm from the oven, accompanied by a bowl of cream cheese dipping sauce, or spread the sauce on top of the warm bread.

dishin' with
DAVID

WRAP IT UP!

Sure, you can present this bread in some plastic wrap and tie it with a ribbon, but here's how to make your gift from your heart even more special: Bake the bread in an attractive baking dish. Put the dipping sauce in a separate plastic container. Wrap them up together. Include the recipe and instructions for rewarming the bread ("Heat in a 350°F oven for 5 to 8 minutes") on an attached gift tag.

breakfast *and* brunch
rise and shine!

WHETHER IT'S ON-THE-RUN crunchy granola for week-days or stacks of buttermilk flapjacks and a pile of apple cider doughnuts for a leisurely Sunday-morning brunch, I've got your menu planned. Pull up a chair; breakfast is on the table.

Sure, breakfast is usually served first thing in the morning, but did you ever think about serving waffles, frittatas, or even French toast for supper? The whole family will love gathering around the dinner table with platters of waffles and some crispy bacon and savory sausage. It's one of the best ways I can think of to end the day.

homemade granola

On mornings when I need some crispy, crunchy goodness to get going, I reach for my home-made granola. Simple to make and bake, it's packed with nutty clusters of oats, raisins, cranber-ries, honey, and cinnamon. This granola is a great way to put some kick into your step and send you out the door smiling.

MAKES 8 TO 9 CUPS

4 cups old-fashioned rolled oats (not quick cooking)
1 cup shredded sweetened coconut
1 cup chopped pecans
½ cup chopped or slivered almonds
3 tablespoons dark brown sugar
2 tablespoons unsalted butter, melted
½ teaspoon ground cinnamon

½ teaspoon kosher salt
¼ teaspoon ground nutmeg
⅓ cup canola oil or applesauce
⅓ cup honey
⅓ cup apple juice
½ cup golden raisins
½ cup pitted and chopped dates
1 cup dried cranberries

Preheat the oven to 350°F.

Stir together the oats, coconut, pecans, almonds, brown sugar, butter, cinnamon, salt, and nutmeg in a large bowl. In a small bowl, whisk together the canola oil, honey, and apple juice.

Pour the oil mixture over the oat mixture and stir with a wooden spoon until the oats and nuts are well coated. Spread the mixture on a large baking sheet and bake, stirring occasionally, for 30 to 40 minutes, until the granola is golden. Remove the granola from the oven and allow it to cool completely, stirring occasionally. Stir in the raisins, dates, and cranberries. Store the gra-nola in an airtight container at room temperature for up to 1 week.

make it your own

- Use maple syrup in place of honey.
- Go nuts with nuts and seeds—add toasted walnuts, hazelnuts, or cashews; sunflower and sesame seeds.
- Dried fruit possibilities are endless—options include chopped cherries, blueberries, apricots, peaches, bananas, figs, and mangoes.
- Build breakfast parfaits by alternating layers of granola and your favorite yogurt in tall glasses. Add a spoon and your breakfast is ready.

ham and egg breakfast wraps

How about a breakfast wrap with a little south-of-the-border zing? I even have two ways to serve it. You can either fill individual tortillas with eggs, ham, and cheese, or put out heaping bowls of all the fixings plus a platter of warmed tortillas so everyone can create their own. Either way, these wraps will keep your gang going all morning long.

MAKES 4 SERVINGS

1 tablespoon unsalted butter

1 garlic clove, minced

3 tablespoons chopped onion

3 tablespoons chopped red bell pepper

Kosher salt and freshly ground black
    pepper

5 large eggs

¾ pound ham, diced

1 tablespoon chopped fresh dill

4 10-inch flour tortillas, warmed

½ cup (2 ounces) grated Cheddar

Salsa (optional)

Melt the butter in a nonstick skillet over medium heat. Add the garlic, onion, and bell pepper and sauté until the vegetables are starting to soften, 2 or 3 minutes. Season with salt and pepper to taste.

While the vegetables are cooking, beat the eggs in a medium bowl. Stir in the diced ham. Pour the egg mixture over the vegetables in the skillet and cook, stirring occasionally, until the eggs are softly set, 3 to 5 minutes. Top with the chopped dill.

Spoon one quarter of the egg mixture down the center of each warm tortilla. Top with the Cheddar. Fold in the short sides of each tortilla and roll it up as you would a burrito. Serve, passing the salsa (if using) on the side.

spinach-tomato frittata

One of my favorite breakfast treats is a savory frittata like this one, made with vine-ripened cherry tomatoes and leafy spinach. In a frittata, the mixings are stirred into the eggs and then everything is poured into a skillet. Once you pop this into the oven, get the coffee started. Breakfast will be ready in no time. Remember, frittatas can be served hot, cold, or at room temperature, so enjoy them anytime.

MAKES 4 SERVINGS

Vegetable oil spray
6 large eggs
⅓ cup diced cherry tomatoes
2 tablespoons chopped fresh basil
1 garlic clove, minced

½ teaspoon kosher salt
½ teaspoon freshly ground black pepper
2 cups coarsely chopped spinach leaves
¼ cup (1 ounce) freshly grated
    Parmigiano-Reggiano

Preheat the oven to 400°F.

Spray an 8-inch ovenproof nonstick skillet with the vegetable oil spray. Heat the skillet over medium heat. While the skillet is heating up, whisk the eggs in a medium bowl until frothy. Stir in the tomatoes, basil, garlic, salt, and pepper.

Add the egg mixture to the skillet and cook without stirring until the eggs begin to set on the bottom, about 1 minute. Top with the spinach leaves. Carefully loosen the edges with a heat-proof spatula and continue to cook for 1 to 2 minutes more.

Transfer the skillet to the oven and bake for 5 to 7 minutes, until the frittata is puffed and golden brown. Place a plate large enough to hold the frittata bottom side up on top of the skillet. With the plate and skillet firmly pressed together, invert the frittata onto the plate. Sprinkle with the Parmigiano-Reggiano. Slice into thin wedges and serve.

make it your own

I don't know about you, but the more colorful ingredients I add to my egg dishes, the better they look—and the better they taste

- broccoli
- onions
- mushrooms
- ham
- sausage

- mozzarella
- bacon (of course)
- bell peppers
- scallions
- feta

- sun-dried tomatoes
- potatoes
- chives
- grated zucchini

egg and sausage strata

When I have guests for brunch, I'd rather spend more time with them than in the kitchen. A make-it-the-night-before breakfast casserole is the perfect solution. With French bread, eggs, six kinds of cheese, sausage, and bell peppers, this strata is a complete meal. What's not to love?

MAKES 4 TO 6 SERVINGS

Vegetable oil spray
1 loaf day-old French bread, cut into 1-inch cubes
1 pound sage pork sausage, casings removed, crumbled
½ cup chopped green bell pepper
½ cup chopped red bell pepper
⅓ cup chopped onion

6 large eggs
3 cups milk
1 teaspoon dry mustard
½ teaspoon kosher salt
½ teaspoon freshly ground black pepper
¼ teaspoon dried oregano
1 8-ounce package shredded Italian cheese blend

Spray a 9 x 13-inch baking dish with the vegetable oil spray. Spread the bread cubes evenly over the bottom of the dish.

Cook the sausage in a large nonstick skillet, stirring occasionally, until no longer pink, about 5 minutes. Add the green peppers, red peppers, and onion and cook about 5 minutes. Drain the fat from the sausage mixture and then evenly spread the sausage mixture over the bread cubes.

Beat the eggs, milk, mustard, salt, pepper, and oregano in a large bowl. Pour the egg mixture evenly over the sausage mixture. Sprinkle the cheese evenly over the surface of the eggs. Cover the baking dish with aluminum foil and refrigerate overnight.

Preheat the oven to 325°F.

Remove the baking dish from the refrigerator while the oven is preheating. Bake, covered, for 1 hour and 15 minutes. Remove the foil and bake for 10 minutes more, or until a knife inserted into the center of the strata comes out clean. Let the strata stand for 10 minutes before serving.

make it your own

Add
- cooked and crumbled bacon
- sautéed mushrooms
- cooked spinach
- crumbled feta
- chopped smoked salmon
- diced tomatoes
- diced prosciutto
- shredded mozzarella

WHAT A TIME-SAVER!

Celery root, that gnarly, knobby vegetable deserves more attention because it's so delicious. Notice that I don't say to peel the skin. A vegetable peeler won't do the trick because the skin is so tough. Instead, using a knife, cut the top and bottom off the celery root. Stand it upright on one of the flat sides. Make vertical slices and cut off the remaining peel all the way around. Cut the celery root into ½-inch pieces.

sage sausage and butternut squash hash

Whenever I hear that someone is making hash, it sounds very old fashioned to me. But as I've learned in the kitchen, everything old can be made new again, especially when a dish features a few unexpected flavors. This one brings together a bunch of sweet and savory ingredients—cubes of butternut squash and celery, dried cranberries, the sharp taste of arugula, and savory sage sausage. Serve it with two sunny-side up eggs and buttered whole grain toast and you have a modern-day hash that is sure to become a new family favorite.

MAKES 8 TO 10 SERVINGS

1 cup slivered almonds

1 pound bulk sage sausage

3 tablespoons unsalted butter

1 red onion, finely diced

2 tablespoons minced garlic

1 large butternut squash (2 to 3 pounds), peeled, seeded, and cut into ½-inch cubes

1 celery root, tough skin removed, diced into ½-inch cubes (page 52)

½ cup chicken stock

4 cups arugula

1 cup dried cranberries

3 tablespoons chopped fresh parsley

1 teaspoon kosher salt

1 teaspoon freshly ground black pepper

Spread the almonds in the bottom of a large, deep sauté pan and toast over medium-high heat, tossing frequently, until they are lightly browned, 3 to 4 minutes. Transfer the almonds to a small bowl and set aside.

Add the sausage to the pan and cook, breaking up any large chunks with a wooden spoon, until the sausage is no longer pink, 5 to 6 minutes. Drain the sausage through a sieve and discard the drippings. Transfer the sausage to a bowl and set aside. Add the butter to the pan and cook just until brown, about 1 minute. Add the red onion and garlic and cook until they are just beginning to soften, 1 to 2 minutes. Add the squash and celery root and continue to cook until the squash is beginning to turn golden, 5 to 6 minutes. Add the chicken stock and cook until the squash is tender, about 3 minutes more.

Add the arugula, cranberries, parsley, salt, and pepper to the pan and stir again. Add the sausage and almonds, stir to combine, and cook just until the mixture is heated through, 4 to 5 minutes. Serve hot.

old-fashioned
buttermilk flapjacks

As a kid, I loved two things about Saturday mornings: cartoons and my mom's buttermilk flap-jacks. Weekends were the only time of the week that Mom didn't work, so she had time to make flapjacks for us. I can still remember her piling two or three flapjacks on my plate along with some bacon and plenty of maple syrup. I loved to dunk bites of pancakes and pieces of bacon into that saucy sweetness. Just follow my simple steps and you'll end up with the kind of light-as-air flapjacks you thought nobody made anymore.

MAKES 12 PANCAKES

1½ cups all-purpose flour

1½ teaspoons baking powder

¾ teaspoon baking soda

¼ teaspoon kosher salt

2 tablespoons sugar

2 large eggs

1¼ cups buttermilk

2 tablespoons canola oil

1 teaspoon pure vanilla extract

Unsalted butter

Whipped butter

Maple syrup

Sift the flour, baking powder, baking soda, salt, and sugar together into a large bowl. In a medium bowl, whisk together the eggs, buttermilk, canola oil, and vanilla. Pour the egg mixture into the flour mixture and mix just until combined. Don't overmix.

Melt a pat of butter in a heavy skillet or on a griddle over medium heat. For each pancake, pour ¼ cup batter in a circle onto the skillet. Cook until bubbles form on the surface and the edges are dry. Flip the pancakes and cook for 2 minutes more. Serve with whipped butter and warm maple syrup.

make it your own

Add

- chocolate chips
- chopped nuts
- blueberries
- sliced bananas
- chopped apples
- sliced strawberries
- peanut butter
- trail mix
- cinnamon
- ½ cup cornmeal for ½ cup flour

amaretto brioche french toast
with cinnamon butter

When I want to serve an extra-special breakfast or brunch for people dear to me, I make this twist on French toast. You'll be amazed at the difference it makes when you use slices of rich, eggy brioche, a splash of amaretto—an almond-flavored Italian liqueur—and a generous dollop of warm cinnamon butter.

MAKES 4 TO 6 SERVINGS

CINNAMON BUTTER
8 tablespoons (1 stick) unsalted butter, at
    room temperature
½ cup confectioners' sugar

½ cup honey
1 teaspoon ground cinnamon

FRENCH TOAST
3 large eggs
1 cup half-and-half
3 tablespoons amaretto
2 teaspoons pure vanilla extract
3 tablespoons brown sugar

2 teaspoons ground cinnamon
1 loaf brioche bread, cut into 1- to 1½-inch
    slices
1 tablespoon unsalted butter
Maple syrup

To make the cinnamon butter, whisk together the butter, confectioners' sugar, honey, and cinnamon in a small bowl until light and fluffy. Set aside.

To make the French toast, whisk together the eggs, half-and-half, amaretto, vanilla, brown sugar, and cinnamon in a 9 x 13-inch baking dish. Add the brioche slices in a single layer and let the mixture stand until the bread has absorbed most of the egg mixture, about 5 minutes.

Meanwhile, melt the butter in a large skillet over medium-high heat. Working in batches, transfer the brioche slices to the skillet. Cook, covered, until they are golden, 1 to 2 minutes per side.

Arrange the slices of French toast on a platter and serve with the cinnamon butter and warm maple syrup.

waffles
with warm mixed berry compote

There are three things I love about my waffles. One, they're crispy on the outsides. Two, they're soft and moist on the insides. Three, there are all of those little squares begging to be filled with sweet ingredients. In this case, the topping is a quick-and-easy warm berry compote. I just realized that there's definitely a fourth thing I love about my waffles. Devouring them.

MAKES 6 WAFFLES

MIXED BERRY COMPOTE

2 teaspoons cornstarch

2 10-ounce packages frozen mixed
    berries, thawed (do not drain)

1 cup sugar

Finely grated zest of 1 lemon

¼ teaspoon ground allspice

¼ teaspoon ground cinnamon

WAFFLES

3 cups all-purpose flour

1 tablespoon plus 1 teaspoon baking
    powder

¼ cup sugar

1 teaspoon kosher salt

4 large eggs, separated

1⅔ cups whole milk

⅓ cup club soda

2 teaspoons pure vanilla extract

4 tablespoons (½ stick) unsalted butter,
    melted

To make the compote, combine the cornstarch and 1 tablespoon water in a small bowl and stir until dissolved. Set aside.

Combine the berries, sugar, lemon zest, allspice, and cinnamon in a medium saucepan and bring to a simmer over medium-high heat. Cook, stirring frequently, until the sugar dissolves. Just before the berry mixture reaches a boil, stir in the cornstarch mixture. Bring to a boil and cook for 1 minute. Remove the pan from the heat. The compote will thicken as it cools. Serve the compote warm or at room temperature.

Preheat the waffle iron.

To make the waffles, sift together the flour, baking powder, sugar, and salt in a large bowl. In a separate large bowl, beat the egg yolks, milk, club soda, and vanilla. Pour the egg mixture into the flour mixture and beat just until combined. Add the melted butter and mix until incorporated.

Wash and dry the beaters. In another large bowl, beat the egg whites until stiff. Using a rubber spatula, carefully fold the egg whites into the batter until no streaks remain.

Spoon the batter into the waffle iron, being careful not to overfill it. Cook until the waffles are golden brown. Serve hot with the berry compote.

christmas-morning french toast casserole

Christmas morning is a time for family fun and, of course, lots of gifts and excitement. No one wants to miss a moment of the celebration, so that's why this casserole is the perfect breakfast solution. First, it's put together the night before so the flavors really get to meld. Second, all you have to do is pop it into the oven. Pretty soon those irresistible warm holiday aromas fill the house and accompany the sounds of laughter as everyone opens their presents. But the best gift is when you and yours are at the table sharing this dish with one another.

MAKES 8 TO 10 SERVINGS

FRENCH TOAST

1 tablespoon unsalted butter, at room temperature

1 loaf French bread, cut into eighteen to twenty 1-inch-thick slices

8 large eggs

2 cups eggnog

1 cup milk

2 tablespoons sugar

1 teaspoon pure vanilla extract

½ teaspoon ground cinnamon

¼ teaspoon ground nutmeg

Pinch of kosher salt

TOPPING

8 tablespoons (1 stick) unsalted butter, at room temperature

1 cup packed light brown sugar

½ to ¾ cup whole red and green maraschino cherries

Maple syrup

1 cup chopped pecans

2 tablespoons light corn syrup

1 teaspoon ground cinnamon

1 teaspoon ground nutmeg

To make the French toast, grease a 9 x 13-inch baking dish with the butter. Arrange the bread slices in the baking dish in two overlapping rows.

Whisk together the eggs, eggnog, milk, sugar, vanilla, cinnamon, nutmeg, and salt in a large bowl. Pour the egg mixture evenly over the bread slices, making sure the bread is well covered. Cover and refrigerate overnight.

Preheat the oven to 350°F.

Remove the baking dish from the refrigerator.

To make the topping, whisk together the butter, brown sugar, pecans, corn syrup, cinnamon, and nutmeg in a medium bowl until thoroughly combined. Sprinkle the topping evenly over the bread.

Bake for 30 to 40 minutes, until lightly browned. Remove the casserole from the oven and decorate with the maraschino cherries in clusters of three to look like holly berries. Serve with maple syrup.

stuffed raisin bread french toast
with pineapple sauce

Breakfast is a perfect time to enjoy sweet and salty flavors together in one recipe. This French toast has a crunchy exterior, and the inside is a creamy, melt-in-your-mouth mixture of ham and cheese. The pop of pineapple makes the perfect finishing touch.

MAKES 8 SERVINGS

FRENCH TOAST

4 large eggs

½ cup heavy cream

¼ cup milk

1 teaspoon pure vanilla extract

1 8-ounce package cream cheese

16 slices raisin bread

1½ pounds thinly sliced ham

3 cups crushed cornflakes cereal

3 tablespoons unsalted butter

PINEAPPLE SAUCE

1½ to 2 cups peeled, cored, and diced
   pineapple

1½ cups fresh pineapple juice

2 tablespoons honey

1 tablespoon light brown sugar

1 tablespoon cornstarch

Preheat the oven to 350°F. Line a baking sheet with parchment paper.

To make the French toast, whisk the eggs, cream, milk, and vanilla in a shallow bowl and set aside.

Spread 1 tablespoon cream cheese on one side of each slice of bread. Divide the ham among 8 bread slices, then top with the remaining 8 bread slices to make sandwiches.

Spread the crushed cornflakes on a plate. Dip each sandwich in the egg mixture and then dredge it in the cornflakes, making sure to coat both sides evenly.

Melt the butter in a large skillet over medium heat. Working in batches, fry the sandwiches until they are golden brown, about 2 minutes per side. Arrange the sandwiches on the prepared baking sheet, overlapping slightly. Bake for 10 to 12 minutes, until hot.

While the French toast is baking, make the pineapple sauce. Heat the pineapple, pineapple juice, honey, and brown sugar in a saucepan. Whisk the cornstarch with 2½ tablespoons water in a small bowl. Stir the cornstarch mixture into the pineapple mixture and bring to a boil—watch carefully so it doesn't boil over. Cook, stirring constantly, until the sauce thickens, about 2 minutes.

Remove the baking sheet from the oven. Serve the French toast with some of the pineapple sauce drizzled over each portion.

broccoli-swiss–canadian bacon crustless quiche

This quiche recipe is far less time-consuming and less complicated than a traditional quiche. Instead of making a piecrust, a quick batter is poured over the broccoli, cheese, and Canadian bacon filling and then baked. Serve it for breakfast or slice it into smaller portions for a brunch buffet.

MAKES 6 SERVINGS

Vegetable oil spray
1 tablespoon extra virgin olive oil
1 small onion, chopped
1 cup (about 5 ounces) Canadian bacon, chopped
1 10-ounce package frozen broccoli florets, thawed and well drained on paper towels
Kosher salt and freshly ground black pepper

2 cups Bisquick
3 cups milk
6 large eggs
1 teaspoon chopped fresh parsley
1 teaspoon fresh thyme
½ teaspoon kosher salt
¼ teaspoon cayenne
1½ cups (6 ounces) shredded Swiss cheese

Preheat the oven to 400°F. Spray an 8-inch square baking dish with the vegetable oil spray.

Heat a sauté pan over medium heat and add the olive oil. When the oil is hot, add the onion. Sauté for 1 minute. Add the Canadian bacon and sauté for 1 minute more. Add the broccoli. Season with salt and pepper to taste. Pour the vegetable-bacon mixture into the prepared baking dish.

Whisk together the Bisquick, milk, eggs, parsley, thyme, salt, and cayenne in a large bowl with a spout until thoroughly blended. Pour the batter evenly over the vegetable-bacon mixture. Sprinkle the Swiss cheese evenly over the top.

Bake for 35 to 40 minutes, until puffy and golden brown. Remove from the oven to a wire rack and let cool for 5 minutes before slicing and serving.

simply the best skillet home fries

I love potatoes. And one of my absolute, and I mean absolute, favorite ways of making them is in the skillet as home fries. Crispy, herby, crunchy, heavenly pieces of potatoes. They're perfect with scrambled, sunny-side-up, or over-easy eggs. Be prepared for people to want seconds, maybe even thirds, so consider doubling the recipe.

MAKES 4 TO 6 SERVINGS

1½ pounds small red potatoes, cut into
   ½-inch cubes
1 tablespoon unsalted butter
1 tablespoon extra virgin olive oil
4 scallions, thinly sliced on the bias

2 garlic cloves, minced
2 tablespoons chopped fresh rosemary
2 tablespoons fresh thyme leaves
2 teaspoons kosher salt
1 teaspoon freshly ground black pepper

Put the potato cubes in a saucepan and cover with water. Bring to a boil and cook for 3 to 4 minutes. Pour the potatoes into a colander and run under cold water to stop the cooking process. Drain well and set aside.

Melt the butter with the olive oil in a 10-inch nonstick skillet over medium-high heat. Add the potatoes and cook, stirring occasionally, until they are browned and crisp on all sides, about 10 minutes. Add the scallions, garlic, rosemary, thyme, salt, and pepper and cook, stirring constantly, until the scallions and garlic soften, 2 or 3 minutes. Transfer the home fries to a platter or serve straight from the skillet.

apple cider doughnuts

When autumn arrives and the leaves start to change colors in Pennsylvania, I always look forward to a day of good old-fashioned apple picking. There's nothing like wandering through acres of apple trees and picking a bushel of different varieties. Many apple orchards also make and sell fresh doughnuts with just-pressed cider. Because doughnuts are best eaten fresh and warm, the ones I buy at farm stands never seem to make it home. So I make my own with cider and bits of fresh, just-picked apples.

MAKES 12 DOUGHNUTS

DOUGHNUTS

2 red apples, such as Cortland or McIntosh, 1½ apples cored and coarsely chopped; the remaining ½ shredded and reserved to mix into the batter

1 tablespoon fresh lemon juice

2½ cups apple cider

3 cups Bisquick

¼ cup milk

1 large egg

2 tablespoons sugar

1 teaspoon pure vanilla extract

¼ teaspoon ground cinnamon

¼ teaspoon ground nutmeg

CIDER GLAZE

½ cup apple cider

3 tablespoons confectioners' sugar, plus more for dusting

Canola oil for frying

To make the doughnuts, toss the chopped apples with the lemon juice in a bowl. Combine the apples and cider in a saucepan over medium heat. Cover and cook until the apples have softened, 8 to 10 minutes. Uncover and continue to cook until the apples are very tender and the cider has reduced to 1 cup, about 5 minutes. Transfer the mixture to a blender or food processor and puree until smooth.

Combine the Bisquick, apple puree, ½ shredded apple, milk, egg, sugar, vanilla, cinnamon, and nutmeg in a large bowl and blend until the mixture begins to come together. Form the dough into a ball and transfer it to a floured work surface. Knead the dough 10 times. Wrap it in plastic wrap and refrigerate for 1 hour.

To make the glaze, bring the apple cider to a boil in a small saucepan. Reduce the heat and let simmer until the mixture has reduced by half, 10 to 15 minutes. Remove from the heat and let cool to room temperature. Once cool, whisk in the confectioners' sugar until dissolved. Set aside while making the doughnuts.

Clip a deep-frying thermometer to the side of a heavy, deep pot. Add 3 to 4 inches of canola oil to the pot and slowly heat the oil to between 350°F and 375°F.

Remove the dough from the refrigerator and unwrap it. Roll out on a floured work surface to a ¼-inch thickness. Using a floured doughnut cutter, cut the dough into 12 rounds. Using a large slotted spoon, carefully lower 3 doughnuts into the hot oil and fry until golden, about 30 seconds on each side. Remove the doughnuts with the slotted spoon and drain on paper towels. Dip one side of the doughnuts into the glaze, then the other side. Don't skimp on the glaze; it's what makes these doughnuts so special. Dust with confectioners' sugar before serving.

soups
══ big bowls of happiness ══

WHEN I WAS A KID, cold, rainy, or snowy days had the winds whipping right through me, chilling me to my bones. What kept me going was knowing that a big bowl of Mom's vegetable soup was waiting for me when I got home. Well, as anyone can plainly see, I'm not exactly a kid anymore. But there's something about a yummy-tasting, tummy-filling bowl of love that still warms me down to my toes. These days, I add a few of my own touches and techniques to Mom's classics.

When it comes to soups with ingredients like beans, lentils, and vegetables, I like to puree just half of the cooked soup, so there's creamy smoothness and some chunkiness in every spoonful. A great contrast in texture and flavor. And don't forget to "think outside the bowl." Use bread bowls (page 6) to serve soup. They make soup extra special, because you get to eat the bowl as well as the soup!

chicken noodle soup

I couldn't include a soup chapter without a recipe for the all-American chicken noodle. This piping-hot and comforting soup is a crowd-pleaser every time. If you don't have any leftover chicken in your fridge, then do what I do: Use a store-bought rotisserie chicken. I get that same deep chicken flavor in the soup with half the work, and warming bowls of chicken noodle soup are just a few simple steps away. Be sure to have a sleeve of crunchy saltines on the side.

MAKES 8 TO 10 SERVINGS

2 tablespoons extra virgin olive oil

1 medium onion, diced

1 large leek, split lengthwise, well rinsed, and sliced crosswise (white and light green parts)

3 medium carrots, cut diagonally into ½-inch slices

3 celery stalks, halved lengthwise and sliced crosswise into ½-inch slices

3 garlic cloves, minced

1 3-pound rotisserie chicken, meat removed and shredded, bones discarded

8 cups low-sodium chicken broth

½ teaspoon dried thyme

1 bay leaf

8 ounces wide egg noodles

2 teaspoons kosher salt

2 teaspoons freshly ground black pepper

½ cup finely chopped fresh parsley

Heat the olive oil in a large stockpot or Dutch oven over medium heat. Add the onion, leek, carrots, celery, and garlic and sauté until the vegetables are soft, 6 to 8 minutes.

Add the shredded chicken, chicken broth, thyme, and bay leaf. Bring the mixture to a boil. Add the noodles, then reduce the heat and simmer until the noodles are tender but still firm to the bite, 8 to 10 minutes. Season with the salt and pepper. Remove the bay leaf, ladle the soup into bowls, and garnish with the parsley.

make it your own

- Add cooked rice, barley, or orzo instead of noodles.
- Add corn, peas, or chopped spinach or tomatoes.
- Stir in 2 lightly beaten eggs at the end of simmering for egg drop soup.
- Add cooked ravioli or tortellini and some Parmesan shavings.
- Stir 1 can Ro-tel Diced Tomatoes & Green Chilies into the simmering broth and top with chopped cilantro and tortilla chips for tortilla soup.

turkey and sausage gumbo

Louisiana is home to some great music and even better food, like hearty gumbo, a thick, soupy stew (or is it a stewy soup?). It's often made with vegetables and chicken, shrimp, crayfish, or duck. My turkey and sausage version has layer upon layer of satisfying savoriness in every bite. Serve small portions in cups or mugs as a first course or larger ones in bowls over steamed rice.

MAKES 8 TO 10 SERVINGS

½ cup plus 1½ teaspoons canola oil

1 pound fresh chorizo sausage or smoked sausage, sliced ½ inch thick

½ cup all-purpose flour

2 cups finely chopped onions

1 cup chopped celery

1 large green bell pepper, cored, seeded, and chopped

2 large garlic cloves, chopped

9 cups low-sodium chicken broth

1 14.5-ounce can diced tomatoes

1 tablespoon tomato paste

1½ cups sliced okra

2 teaspoons kosher salt

1 teaspoon dried thyme

2 bay leaves

¼ teaspoon red pepper flakes

¼ teaspoon cayenne

3 teaspoons hot sauce

3 cups cooked and diced turkey

4 cups cooked white rice

Heat 1½ teaspoons of the canola oil in a large stockpot or Dutch oven. Add the chorizo and cook until it is cooked through, 6 to 8 minutes. Drain the chorizo, reserving ½ cup of the pan drippings. Set aside the chorizo.

Combine the reserved drippings, the remaining ½ cup canola oil, and the flour in a large saucepan. Cook over medium-low heat, stirring slowly and constantly, until the mixture is the color of peanut butter, 10 to 15 minutes. The roux will start to turn color after 10 to 12 minutes. Be careful not to burn or scorch it.

Add the onions, celery, bell pepper, and garlic to the pot and cook until the vegetables are beginning to soften, about 5 minutes. Add the brown roux and stir to incorporate. Slowly add the chicken broth and whisk until no lumps remain.

Add the tomatoes, tomato paste, okra, salt, thyme, bay leaves, red pepper flakes, cayenne, and hot sauce. Bring the mixture to a simmer and cook, stirring occasionally, for 30 minutes.

Add the turkey and chorizo and continue to simmer for about 15 minutes. Discard the bay leaves and serve the gumbo in bowls over a scoop of rice.

cream of broccoli soup
with cheddar and bacon

No matter how many times you tell your kids that broccoli is just like little trees, they'll still find a way to bury it under the mashed potatoes and never touch it. If you want your kids to eat broccoli, use it in a soup that includes other favorites. Did somebody mention Cheddar and bacon? After they try it once, this is a soup they'll ask you to make again and again.

MAKES 6 TO 8 SERVINGS

1 tablespoon plus 2 teaspoons kosher salt

1 large head broccoli, stems and florets separated and finely chopped

6 bacon slices, cooked (page 137) and crumbled; 2 tablespoons drippings reserved

1 medium onion, chopped

1 garlic clove, minced

3 tablespoons unsalted butter

3 tablespoons all-purpose flour

1 cup whole milk

1 cup light cream

3 cups low-sodium chicken broth

¾ cup (3 ounces) shredded Cheddar

1 teaspoon freshly ground black pepper

2 tablespoons chopped fresh chives

Prepare a large bowl of ice cubes and cold water. Bring a large pot of water to a boil. Add 1 tablespoon salt. Add the broccoli and cook just until the broccoli is bright green, about 2 minutes. Drain the broccoli in a colander and then immediately plunge it into the ice water to stop the cooking process. Drain and set aside.

Add the onion and garlic to the skillet with the bacon drippings. Sauté over medium-high heat until the onion has softened, 2 to 3 minutes. Set aside.

Melt the butter in a large stockpot or Dutch oven. Add the flour and cook for 3 to 4 minutes, stirring constantly, to make a light roux. Whisk in the milk and cream. Cook over medium heat, whisking constantly, until the mixture has thickened, 10 to 12 minutes. Add the chicken broth. Stir in the broccoli, onion-garlic mixture, and cooked bacon.

Transfer half of the soup to a food processor or blender and puree until smooth. Return the soup to the pot and heat over medium heat just until hot. Add the Cheddar, 2 teaspoons salt, and pepper. Ladle the soup into bowls and garnish with the chives before serving.

creamy tomato soup
with grilled cheese croutons

What is it about the combination of tomato soup and a grilled cheese sandwich that puts it near to the top of everyone's list of all-American comfort foods? There are even restaurants and food trucks that specialize in this perfect union of savory soup and classic sandwich.

One day, while dipping a piece of my grilled cheese sandwich into my bowl of soup, I dropped it in. Never one to let a grilled cheese sandwich go to waste, I spooned it out and ate it. It was so good that I purposely dropped in another piece. And another. And then it hit me: Why not make grilled cheese sandwich croutons and sprinkle them on top of the soup?

MAKES 6 TO 8 SERVINGS

CREAMY TOMATO SOUP

2 tablespoons unsalted butter

2 tablespoons extra virgin olive oil

1 large onion, chopped

1 teaspoon kosher salt, plus more to taste

1 teaspoon freshly ground black pepper,
   plus more to taste

1 tablespoon minced garlic

2 tablespoons all-purpose flour

1 28-ounce can whole peeled tomatoes

2 tablespoons tomato paste

1 teaspoon sugar

3 cups vegetable broth

½ cup heavy cream

GRILLED CHEESE CROUTONS
(MAKES 60)

8 tablespoons (1 stick) unsalted butter, at
   room temperature

½ teaspoon fresh thyme leaves

6 thin slices sandwich bread

1 cup (4 ounces) shredded sharp Cheddar

To make the soup, heat the butter and olive oil in a large stockpot or Dutch oven over low heat. Add the onion, salt, and pepper. Cook, stirring occasionally, until the onion is soft, 6 to 8 minutes. Add the garlic and cook for 2 minutes more. Sprinkle with the flour to make a roux, and stir constantly for 3 minutes more.

Stir in the tomatoes, tomato paste, sugar, and vegetable broth. Bring the mixture to a boil, then reduce the heat, cover, and simmer for 30 minutes. Taste the soup and add salt and pepper, if necessary. Remove the soup from the heat and allow it to cool slightly. Working in batches, puree the soup in a food processor or blender. (Alternatively, puree the soup in the pot with an immersion blender.) Return the soup to the pot and stir in the cream. Reheat over low heat just until hot. Do not boil.

To make the croutons, heat a grill pan or a large skillet over medium-high heat.

Mash together the butter and thyme in a small bowl until well blended.

Spread one side of each of the bread slices with the thyme butter. Place 3 slices, butter side down, in the hot pan. Top each slice with the cheese, then the remaining bread slices, butter side up. Grill until the sandwiches are toasted and browned and the cheese has melted, 3 to 5 minutes per side. Remove the sandwiches from the pan and allow them to cool slightly. Cut the sandwiches into 1-inch squares.

Serve the soup, accompanied by the Grilled Cheese Croutons.

dishin' with DAVID

SO, YOU THINK YOU KNOW HOW TO MAKE A GRILLED CHEESE SANDWICH?

Well, I sure thought I did! When "cheese wiz" and cookbook author Laura Werlin appeared on *In the Kitchen with David,* she shared the secret behind a gooey, toasty grilled cheese. It's all about balance—evenly melted cheese and properly toasted bread. Make sure the bread isn't too thick or the cheese won't melt evenly. Shred the cheese (this goes for any kind of cheese you use) using a box grater—no slabs or slices—for even melting. Mix together some of the cheese and room-temperature butter, then spread it on the bread before the bread goes into the pan for a crispy, crunchy exterior. If melted in the pan, the butter will burn and so will your bread. Use the remaining shredded cheese in the sandwich.

make it your own

Add one or more of the following to basic grilled cheese sandwiches:

- sliced tomatoes
- jalapeños
- caramelized onions
- sliced ham or roast beef
- cooked bacon
- shredded leftover chicken
- sliced apples or pears
- guacamole
- bread 'n' butter pickles

timeless minestrone soup

On a cold, wintry day when I first moved to Philadelphia, I was out running some errands and decided to stop at an Italian restaurant for lunch. After scanning the menu for something that would instantly warm me up, I ordered the minestrone soup. I wasn't prepared for how rich, hearty, and loaded with vegetables it was. I can still remember how the waiter spooned on some grated Parmesan with a flourish. The soup was so good that I sopped up the last drops with slices of fresh, crusty Italian bread.

MAKES 8 TO 10 SERVINGS

2 cups dried kidney beans, picked over and soaked overnight, or 1 15.5-ounce can kidney beans, rinsed and drained

2 tablespoons extra virgin olive oil

1 small onion, chopped

3 garlic cloves, minced

1 carrot, diced

1 celery stalk, diced

1 medium zucchini, diced

1 small yellow squash, diced

1 cup 1-inch green bean pieces

2 14.5-ounce cans diced tomatoes

3 tablespoons tomato paste

5 cups vegetable broth

1 teaspoon dried basil

½ teaspoon dried oregano

2 cups cooked elbow macaroni

2 teaspoons kosher salt

1 teaspoon freshly ground black pepper

½ teaspoon cayenne

Freshly grated Parmigiano-Reggiano

Put the kidney beans in a large stockpot or Dutch oven and add enough water to cover them by 2 inches. Bring to a boil, partially cover the pot, and reduce to a simmer. Cook until the beans are tender, about 1 hour. Drain the beans and set aside.

Heat the olive oil in the same pot. Add the onion, garlic, carrot, and celery and cook until the vegetables are lightly browned, about 5 minutes. Add the zucchini, yellow squash, green beans, tomatoes, and tomato paste. Stir in the vegetable broth and 2 cups water.

Add the kidney beans, basil, and oregano to the pot. Bring to a simmer and cook until the vegetables are tender, about 35 minutes. Add the cooked macaroni and heat through, about 5 minutes. Taste and season the soup with the salt, black pepper, and cayenne. Serve hot or warm and pass the Parmigiano-Reggiano.

butternut squash soup
with pumpkin butter

At the first nip in the air, I start looking for fresh butternut squash at farmers' markets, just so I can make this soup. Considered a Thanksgiving classic, this versatile and universally loved soup is simply too tasty to enjoy only once a year. Now that peeled and precut butternut squash is available in grocery stores year-round, you can make this easy three-step—roast, blend, and simmer—soup anytime you like. Like apple or pear butter, pumpkin butter is gently cooked with some sugar until it's smooth and has a buttery texture. Look for pumpkin butter near the jams and jellies in your grocery store.

MAKES 6 TO 8 SERVINGS

Vegetable oil spray
1 2-pound butternut squash, halved
  lengthwise and seeded
2 cups low-sodium chicken broth
½ teaspoon ground cinnamon
½ teaspoon dried marjoram
½ teaspoon dried thyme

Pinch of grated nutmeg
1 cup milk or half-and-half
Kosher salt and freshly ground black
  pepper
1 10-ounce jar pumpkin butter
Chopped pistachio nuts

Preheat the oven to 375°F. Spray a 9 x 13-inch baking dish with the vegetable oil spray.

Place the squash halves, cut side down, in the prepared dish. Pierce the skin sides several times with a fork. Bake until the squash is tender, about 45 minutes. Set aside until cool enough to handle.

Using a large spoon, scrape the flesh from the cooked squash into a food processor. Discard the skins. Add 1½ cups of the chicken broth, the cinnamon, marjoram, thyme, and nutmeg and puree until smooth. Transfer the puree to a large saucepan. Whisk the milk into the soup over medium heat. If you prefer a thinner consistency, add the remaining broth. Season to taste with salt and pepper.

Ladle the soup into warmed bowls. Top with a dollop of pumpkin butter and sprinkle with chopped pistachio nuts before serving.

make it your own

GO NUTS OVER BUTTERNUT

- Roll diced squash in a bit of canola oil and ground cinnamon. Spread on a sheet pan, sprinkle with brown sugar, and bake at 375°F for 15 to 20 minutes. Add these sweet bits of squash when pureeing the soup.
- Substitute crème fraîche or sour cream for the pumpkin butter.
- Serve the soup chilled or warm in shot glasses as a party starter.

IT'S BETTER WITH A LITTLE BUTTER

Why do creamy soups taste so much creamier in restaurants? "The secret in restaurants is that we finish it with some butter," New York chef/restaurateur David Burke told me. "Melt a generous pat of butter into the soup just before serving. It coats the palate, gives you a nice aroma, and smoothes out the flavors."

loaded baked potato soup

Since I love twice-baked potatoes so much, I got to thinking: What if I combined all my favorite ingredients—potatoes, Cheddar, sour cream, and bacon—into a creamy and scrumptious soup? And then I topped each serving with more of the same flavors? Violà! It's perfection in a bowl. As a final touch, I sprinkle each serving with some freshly ground black peppercorns.

MAKES 8 TO 10 SERVINGS

4 medium baking potatoes

8 tablespoons (1 stick) unsalted butter

1 cup all-purpose flour

6 cups milk

1 cup (4 ounces) shredded extra sharp Cheddar

2 teaspoons kosher salt, plus more to taste

1½ teaspoons garlic powder

1 teaspoon freshly ground black pepper, plus more to taste

1 cup (8 ounces) sour cream

¾ cup chopped scallions (white and light green parts only)

6 bacon slices, cooked (page 137) and crumbled

Preheat the oven to 400°F.

Pierce the potatoes several times with a fork. Bake the potatoes until they are tender, about 1 hour. Cool the potatoes and peel them. Cut 3 of the potatoes into medium dice; coarsely mash the remaining potato.

Melt the butter in a large Dutch oven over medium-low heat. Add the flour and whisk until smooth. Gradually whisk in the milk. Cook the mixture over medium heat until it is thick, 8 to 10 minutes. Add the diced and mashed potatoes, ¾ cup of the Cheddar, salt, garlic powder, and pepper. Stir until the cheese melts, then remove the pot from the heat and stir in the sour cream and ½ cup of the scallions.

Return the pot to low heat and cook just until heated through (do not boil). Season the soup with salt and pepper, if necessary. Ladle the soup into bowls and garnish with the remaining Cheddar and scallions, and the bacon. Garnish with some coarsely ground black pepper.

italian wedding soup

I first enjoyed this Italian-American soup at the wedding reception of some dear friends. When a bowl was placed in front of me, I couldn't believe how good it smelled. I was delighted to find mini meatballs underneath the spinach in the rich chicken broth. I was even more delighted to learn that the airy, delicate meatballs were made with chicken. The soup was such an exceptional blend of flavors and textures that I immediately learned how to make it. Now you can, too.

MAKES 6 TO 8 SERVINGS

MEATBALLS

1 pound ground chicken

½ cup finely chopped onion

½ teaspoon minced garlic

2 tablespoons freshly grated Parmigiano-Reggiano

2 tablespoons dried bread crumbs

1 tablespoon mayonnaise

1 large egg yolk

1 teaspoon Italian seasoning

1 teaspoon minced fresh parsley

½ teaspoon kosher salt

¼ teaspoon freshly ground black pepper

SOUP

2 tablespoons extra virgin olive oil

1 small onion, chopped

2 carrots, chopped

2 celery stalks, chopped

8 cups low-sodium chicken broth

½ teaspoon minced fresh thyme

2 bay leaves

¾ cup orzo

1 10-ounce package frozen chopped spinach, thawed, drained, and squeezed dry

Freshly grated Parmigiano-Reggiano

To make the meatballs, preheat the oven to 400°F. Line a baking sheet with parchment paper.

Combine the chicken, onion, garlic, Parmigiano-Reggiano, bread crumbs, mayonnaise, egg yolk, Italian seasoning, parsley, salt, and pepper in a medium bowl. Using clean hands, mix thoroughly until well combined.

Using clean hands, form the chicken mixture into small balls, no more than 1 inch round. They should be small. Place the meatballs on the prepared baking sheet. Bake the meatballs until they are cooked through, 5 to 8 minutes. Let the meatballs cool on the baking sheet.

To make the soup, heat the olive oil in a large stockpot or Dutch oven. Add the onion, carrots, and celery, and sauté just until soft, 6 to 8 minutes. Add the chicken broth, thyme, and bay leaves and bring to a simmer. Simmer for 15 to 20 minutes. Add the orzo and simmer until tender but still firm to the bite, 6 to 8 minutes. Add the meatballs and spinach to the soup and heat through, 5 to 8 minutes. Remove and discard the bay leaves. Ladle the soup into warm bowls. Garnish with grated Parmigiano-Reggiano before serving.

white bean and ham soup

Don't know what to do with a leftover ham bone after the holidays? It's the perfect opportunity to make this soup. That leftover bone is loaded with flavor, but rather than attempting to pick those bits of ham off the bone to put into the pot, let the simmering soup do the job.

When it comes to beans, it seems that cooks can be divided into two groups—those who soak their dried beans for eight hours before cooking them and those who don't. I tend to fit into the no-soak group, because I always find I'm short on time. And when I want savory bean and ham soup, I want it as quickly as possible. Here's how I make it.

MAKES 6 TO 8 SERVINGS

1 pound dried Great Northern beans	1 onion, chopped
8 cups water	1 teaspoon minced garlic
½ teaspoon kosher salt	1 teaspoon dry mustard
5 cups low-sodium chicken broth	2 bay leaves
2 to 3 pounds of ham shank	Kosher salt and freshly ground black
3 carrots, chopped	pepper
1 celery stalk, chopped	2 scallions, finely sliced

Put the beans in a colander and rinse under cool water, discarding any pebbles or broken and discolored beans. Bring the water to a boil. Add the beans and the salt, and then remove the pot from the heat. Let the beans sit in the hot water for 1 hour, then drain and return the beans to the pot.

Heat the chicken broth and beans in the same pot over medium heat. Stir in the ham bone, carrots, celery, onion, garlic, mustard, and bay leaves. Bring the soup to a boil, then immediately reduce the heat to low and let simmer for 1 hour. If the soup seems dry, add ½ to 1 cup water as necessary.

Using tongs, remove the ham bone to a plate. When it's cool enough to handle, pull off any remaining bits of meat and add them to the soup. Simmer for 30 additional minutes. Season with salt and pepper. Ladle the soup into bowls, garnish with the scallions, and serve hot.

dishin' with DAVID

COLD BOWLS, NOT-SO-HOT SOUP

By the time hot soup gets to the table, it's often just warm. The culprit is usually cold bowls. Before serving, heat your soup bowls by setting them on the back of the stove while the oven is on or using them warm from the dishwasher. For larger crowds, keep the soup hot in a slow cooker with the lid slightly ajar. Completely covering cream soups causes excess heat to build up and the soups can break down.

hearty lentil soup
with bacon

Now this is a real stick-to-your-ribs soup. It's so filling, satisfying, and full of robust flavors that it makes me want to lick the bowl. Since lentils don't require overnight or quick soaking like dried beans, you can have this soup on the dinner table in less than an hour. These little morsels absorb the flavors of whatever ingredients they're cooked with. Full of smoky bacon, pungent garlic, and plenty of herbs, this ideal cold-weather soup tastes even better when reheated the next day.

MAKES 8 TO 10 SERVINGS

1 tablespoon extra virgin olive oil

9 slices bacon, cut into ½-inch pieces

1 cup chopped onion

1 cup chopped celery

1 cup chopped carrots

3 garlic cloves, minced

10 cups low-sodium chicken broth

1 cup water

2 cups brown lentils

3 sprigs fresh thyme

1 bay leaf

Salt and freshly ground black pepper, to taste

2 tablespoons chopped fresh parsley

Heat the olive oil in a large Dutch oven over medium-high heat. Add the bacon and cook for 2 to 3 minutes. Add the onion, celery, and carrots and cook for another 2 to 3 minutes, stirring occasionally. Lower the heat to medium. Add the garlic, cover, and continue cooking for 6 to 8 minutes, until the bacon is crisp and the vegetables are tender.

Uncover the pot and add 8 cups of the chicken broth, the water, lentils, thyme, and bay leaf. Bring to a boil, then reduce the heat and simmer for 45 minutes, stirring occasionally, until the lentils are tender. Remove and discard the thyme sprigs and bay leaf. Allow the soup to cool slightly.

Transfer one third of the soup to a food processor or blender and puree until smooth. Return the soup to the pot. Bring the soup to a simmer, adding more broth if it seems too thick. Season the soup with additional salt and pepper to taste. Ladle the soup into bowls and garnish with the parsley before serving.

Make it your own

- Add a smoked turkey wing or leg to the soup while it's cooking.
- Add 2 cups chopped spinach or kale during the last 10 minutes of cooking.
- Use red, yellow, or green lentils in place of brown.
- Add 1 cup cooked orzo or small macaroni.
- Serve with a dollop of yogurt on top.
- Garnish with chopped avocado.

new england clam chowder

A good friend of mine on Cape Cod keeps telling me, "David, it's not pronounced 'chow-der' but 'chow-dah.'" It's good on a frigid winter's day or before a seafood dinner during the summer. Bursting with creaminess, bacon, clams, herbs, and spices, any way you say it, this classic is pronounced "fantastic."

This dish deserves individual sourdough bread bowls (page 6), and so do your guests.

MAKES 6 TO 8 SERVINGS

1 pound bacon slices, cut into ½-inch pieces

8 tablespoons (1 stick) unsalted butter

1 large onion, finely chopped

4 garlic cloves, minced

4 celery stalks, finely chopped

¾ cup all-purpose flour

1 46-ounce can clam juice

4 large baking potatoes, peeled and cut into small dice

2 teaspoons fresh thyme leaves

2 bay leaves

2 dozen littleneck clams, steamed, shucked, and chopped, or 2 10-ounce cans chopped clams with their juices

4 cups heavy cream

1½ teaspoons kosher salt

½ teaspoon freshly ground black pepper

½ teaspoon Old Bay Seasoning

½ cup chopped fresh parsley

2 tablespoons minced scallions (white and light green parts)

Oyster crackers

Put the bacon into a cold, not preheated, stockpot or Dutch oven over medium heat so it cooks. Let the bacon cook for 3 minutes on each side. Remove the cooked bacon to paper towels to drain. Discard all but 2 tablespoons of the bacon drippings. When cool enough to handle, crumble the bacon.

Add the butter to the pot with the reserved drippings. Add the onion, garlic, and celery and cook over medium heat until the vegetables are soft, about 10 minutes. Stir in the flour with a wooden spoon. Gradually whisk in the clam juice and cook, whisking constantly, until the mixture is thick and creamy, 10 to 12 minutes. Stir in the potatoes, thyme, and bay leaves and simmer the mixture over low heat for 20 minutes. Stir in the clams and the reserved bacon and simmer until the potatoes are tender, 15 to 20 minutes.

Slowly stir in the cream and heat just until the chowder is heated through (do not boil). Remove the chowder from the heat. Remove and discard the bay leaves. Season the chowder with the salt and pepper. Ladle the chowder into bowls and sprinkle with Old Bay Seasoning. Serve the chowder garnished with parsley and scallions and pass a bowl of oyster crackers.

salads
green goodness

I'M TALKING CRISPY, crunchy, colorful, vibrant, fresh, bright, fruity, sweet, tart, tangy, creamy, tantalizing, and satisfying salads. Whether they're served as sides or main courses, the varieties are limitless and easy to prepare. They can be as simple as a wedge of iceberg lettuce with a bacon and blue cheese dressing, as colorful as pasta salad, or as seasonal as a summery corn salad. Salads can be made with greens, meats, fruits, nuts, cooked vegetables, cheeses, and pasta, and then tossed with so many different dressings.

Foodies, here you'll find a salad for every taste and kind of meal. And you'll love every single one.

spinach salad
with warm bacon dressing

Baby spinach is one of the most tender, flavorful, and nutrient-rich greens you can eat. Warm bacon dressing offers slightly smoky, slightly crunchy, slightly tangy flavors that work perfectly with this leafy green treat.

MAKES 4 SERVINGS

1 11-ounce package baby spinach
½ red onion, sliced
8 ounces button mushrooms, sliced
¼ cup dried cranberries
8 bacon slices, cooked (page 137) and crumbled; 3 tablespoons drippings reserved
3 tablespoons red wine vinegar

1 teaspoon sugar
½ teaspoon Dijon mustard
2 tablespoons chopped fresh basil
Kosher salt and freshly ground black pepper
6 hard-boiled eggs, sliced
½ cup (2 ounces) Pecorino Romano shavings

Toss together the spinach, red onion, mushrooms, and cranberries in a large bowl. Set aside.

Whisk together the bacon drippings, vinegar, sugar, mustard, and basil in a saucepan over low heat. Season with a pinch each of salt and pepper.

Drizzle the warm dressing over the spinach salad and toss to combine. Add the crumbled bacon and the eggs. Top with the pecorino shavings before serving.

make it your own

- Toss the warm bacon dressing with potatoes, shredded cabbage, or blanched green beans.
- Use the dressing with grilled chicken, shrimp, or fish.

caesar salad

At one time, fancy restaurants made a big deal out of preparing Caesar salads tableside. Guests *oohed* and *aahed* while servers whisked the dressing ingredients into a creamy topping for the chopped romaine. As a final flourish, croutons and grated Parmesan were added. Now, this classic salad can be found on menus everywhere—ringside shows are a thing of the past—and you can choose from many add-ons, including grilled shrimp, chicken, and steak. I've even seen them made with grilled romaine.

I make my Caesar salads with an untraditional twist: I leave the romaine leaves whole and add some shredded carrots and hard-boiled egg with the garlic-mustard dressing drizzled on top. It's a showstopper!

MAKES 4 SERVINGS

CROUTONS
2 tablespoons extra virgin olive oil

1 garlic clove, minced with a pinch of salt
   to make a paste

1 teaspoon minced fresh parsley

1 cup day-old bread cubes

DRESSING
Juice of 1 lemon

1 tablespoon Dijon mustard

2 large egg yolks from pasteurized eggs

2 garlic cloves, minced

1 teaspoon kosher salt

2 anchovy fillets

¼ cup extra virgin olive oil

2 tablespoons freshly grated Parmigiano-
   Reggiano

SALAD
18 to 24 crisp, narrow leaves from 2 heads
   romaine lettuce

1 large hard-boiled egg, quartered

Freshly grated Parmigiano-Reggiano

To make the croutons, preheat the oven to 350°F.

Heat the olive oil in a skillet over medium-high heat. Add the garlic paste and sauté for 30 seconds. Add the parsley and bread cubes and toss to combine. Transfer the bread cubes to a baking sheet and bake until they are toasted, about 10 minutes. Set aside.

To make the dressing, combine the lemon juice, mustard, egg yolks, garlic, salt, and anchovies in a blender and pulse to combine. With the blender running, gradually add the olive oil in a steady stream and blend until the oil is incorporated and the dressing is emulsified. Add the Parmesan and pulse to combine.

To compose the salad, place the romaine in a salad bowl and toss with just enough dressing to coat the leaves. Divide the romaine among four salad plates. Add the croutons, a hard-boiled egg quarter, and Parmesan. Pass additional cheese so each person can add more as needed.

iceberg wedges
with bacon and blue cheese dressing

When I make an all-American steak dinner at home, I pull out all the stops. The meal always starts with this classic steak house salad. It's so easy to make and always draws raves. It's crunchy, flavorful, and includes the tangy zing of blue cheese dressing. Be sure to follow the salad with the Marinated Rib-Eye Steaks with Gorgonzola Butter (page 181), Over-the-Top Twice-Baked Potatoes (page 108), and Beer-Battered Onion Rings with Horseradish-Dill Dipping Sauce (page 111). How good does that sound?

MAKES 6 SERVINGS

BLUE CHEESE DRESSING

1½ cups mayonnaise

2 tablespoons fresh lemon juice

1½ teaspoons freshly ground black pepper

1½ teaspoon hot sauce

1 cup crumbled blue cheese

½ cup buttermilk

½ teaspoon kosher salt

½ teaspoon freshly ground black pepper

SALAD

1 large head iceberg lettuce, cut into 6 wedges

½ pound thick-cut bacon slices, cooked (page 137) and crumbled

1 large hard-boiled egg, chopped

½ red onion, diced

To make the dressing, whisk the mayonnaise, lemon juice, pepper, and hot sauce in a medium bowl. Stir in the blue cheese. Thin the dressing to the desired consistency with the buttermilk (you may not need all the buttermilk). Season with the salt and pepper. (Dressing can be made 1 day ahead. Cover and refrigerate.)

Arrange each iceberg wedge on a salad plate and spoon some of the dressing and cooked bacon over the wedges. Sprinkle the salads with the hard-boiled egg and the red onion.

chicken salad

with apples, celery, and cherries

Chicken salad often gets a bad rap. It's sometimes made with too much mayonnaise, leaving it gloppy. But knowing how popular chicken salad is, I made it my mission to rescue it from a sea of sameness and to ramp up its flavors. I decided to add apples, celery, and cherries for some real texture, color, and flavor. And cut *waaaay* back on the mayo. Now this dish is both delicious and pretty.

MAKES 4 TO 6 SERVINGS

3 cups cooked and shredded chicken

½ cup diced celery

½ cup peeled and diced apple

¼ cup dried cherries

¼ cup chopped pecans or walnuts (optional)

2 to 3 tablespoons finely chopped red onion

4 to 6 tablespoons mayonnaise

1 tablespoon apple cider vinegar

2 teaspoons fresh lemon juice

¼ teaspoon dry mustard

Kosher salt

⅛ teaspoon freshly ground black pepper

1 tablespoon minced fresh parsley

Combine the chicken, celery, apple, cherries, pecans (if using), and red onion in a large bowl.

Whisk together the mayonnaise, vinegar, lemon juice, and mustard in a small bowl. Season with salt and the pepper.

Pour the mayonnaise mixture over the chicken mixture and toss until the chicken is evenly coated. Sprinkle with the parsley before serving.

make it your own

- Spoon the chicken salad on top of a bed of mixed greens.
- Spread on wraps and roll up burrito style.
- Substitute raisins for the cranberries.
- Scoop onto avocado halves or into hollowed-out tomatoes.

italian pasta salad

This colorful salad is ideal for summertime neighborhood gatherings, family picnics, and outdoor barbecues. Pieces of Italian salamis, sun-dried tomatoes, and mozzarella are tossed with tricolored pasta for a one-bowl antipasto. When looking to add color to your meals, turn to this recipe.

MAKES 6 TO 8 SERVINGS

2 tablespoons Kosher salt, plus more to taste

1 pound tricolored rotini or fusilli

2 garlic cloves, finely chopped

1 tablespoon Dijon mustard

2 tablespoons balsamic vinegar

½ cup extra virgin olive oil

¼ pound Genoa salami, cut into ½-inch cubes

½ pound sweet soppressata, thinly sliced and cut into julienne strips

½ cup (1 ounce) sun-dried tomatoes (not oil-packed), soaked in hot water for 5 minutes, well drained, and chopped

8 ounces mozzarella, cut into ½-inch cubes

¾ cup pitted black olives, drained and chopped

1 cup packed fresh basil leaves, thinly sliced

¼ cup freshly grated Parmigiano-Reggiano

Freshly ground black pepper

Bring a large pot of water to the boil. Add 2 tablespoons salt. Add the rotini and cook, stirring occasionally, until tender but still firm to the bite. Drain the pasta in a colander and set aside to cool.

Put the garlic, mustard, vinegar, olive oil, and salt to taste in a lidded jar and shake vigorously.

Combine the pasta, salami, soppressata, sun-dried tomatoes, mozzarella, olives, basil, and Parmesan in a large bowl. Toss well with some of the dressing. Add more dressing and salt and pepper to taste. Cover and refrigerate for at least 1 hour before serving.

dishin' with DAVID

PASTA SALAD WITH A TWIST

Chop all the ingredients and make the dressing before cooking the pasta. Once the pasta is cooked and cooled, you can put this salad together in minutes.

When authors and television hosts Josh Kilmer-Purcell and Brent Ridge, also known as The Fabulous Beekman Boys, became city slickers turned farmers, they learned a lot about ingredients.

"Everyone thinks so much of food and cooking culture is finding specific ingredients. 'I have to get South African kumquats in order to make a gourmet meal.' But so much of great cooking is not about what you can get, but what you can't get. If you can't get tomatoes because they're not ripe yet, you probably shouldn't be making marinara sauce. Then you really appreciate those dishes."

fresh summer corn salad

One of my favorite summer memories is of my grandmother "Burnzie's" garden with its green stalks of corn. I was always tall, but by summer's end, those giant corn stalks always made me feel a lot shorter. Corn can give so many dishes a fresh summer spin. Adding other flavors makes this salad the perfect side or starter dish with burgers, steaks, fish, and seafood. Try cooking some fresh corn over the charcoal. Oh my word! That is a wow.

MAKES 4 SERVINGS

1 teaspoon sugar
1 teaspoon plus 2 teaspoons red wine vinegar
6 fresh ears of corn, shucked
1 avocado, pitted, peeled, and chopped
8 to 10 cherry tomatoes, halved
1 garlic clove, finely minced
1 tablespoon extra virgin olive oil

½ teaspoon kosher salt
½ teaspoon freshly ground black pepper
3 cups torn mixed lettuces, such as romaine, red leaf, and butter
½ red onion, thinly sliced
1 cucumber, thinly sliced
½ cup crumbled feta
½ cup julienned fresh basil leaves

Bring a large pot of water to a boil. Add the sugar and 1 teaspoon of the vinegar to the boiling water. Add the corn and bring the water to a rolling boil. Cover the pot, remove it from the heat, and let the corn sit for 10 minutes. Remove the corn from the pot. When the corn is cool enough to handle, use a knife to slice the kernels off the cobs.

Toss the corn kernels, avocado, tomatoes, garlic, the remaining 2 teaspoons vinegar, the olive oil, salt, and pepper in a medium bowl.

Divide the lettuce among four plates. Top each plate with red onion and cucumber. Spoon a mound of the corn mixture on top. Sprinkle on the feta and basil before serving.

three-bean salad

We usually don't associate beans with salads, but they add great texture and flavor. And they come in so many different varieties—cannellini, navy, pinto, butter—in addition to the ones below. If you're looking for a quick alternative to baked beans, try this simple salad.

MAKES 8 SERVINGS

1 15-ounce can red kidney beans, rinsed and drained

1 15-ounce can black beans, rinsed and drained

1 15-ounce can chickpeas, rinsed and drained

½ cup diced green bell pepper

2 cups diced celery

½ cup diced red onion

¼ cup extra virgin olive oil

3 tablespoons fresh lime juice

1 tablespoon apple cider vinegar

1½ teaspoons kosher salt

1 teaspoon ground cumin

½ teaspoon cayenne

1 teaspoon minced garlic

¼ teaspoon freshly ground black pepper

½ cup chopped fresh cilantro

Combine the kidney beans, black beans, chickpeas, bell pepper, celery, and red onion in a large bowl. In a small bowl, whisk together the olive oil, lime juice, vinegar, salt, cumin, cayenne, garlic, black pepper, and cilantro.

Pour the olive oil mixture over the bean mixture and toss to coat. Chill the salad for at least 2 hours before serving.

creamy potato salad
with bacon

Do you know what summer means to me? Eating outdoors—even if it's in my own backyard—picnics, barbecues, you name it. And one dish in particular comes to mind—potato salad. The challenge for us foodies is always to get creative with even the most classic of dishes. So I step up my potato salad by adding some diced vegetables, Dijon mustard, and crispy bacon. Leftovers? Not a chance.

MAKES 6 TO 8 SERVINGS

3 pounds Red Bliss potatoes (about 24 potatoes)

1 tablespoon plus 1 teaspoon kosher salt

1½ cups mayonnaise

2 tablespoons Dijon mustard

½ cup diced onions

¼ cup diced carrots

¼ cup diced celery

1½ teaspoons freshly ground black pepper

¼ cup chopped fresh parsley

8 bacon slices, cooked (page 137) and crumbled

Cut the potatoes in quarters and place them in a large pot. Add enough cold water to cover them completely. Bring the water to a boil and add 1 tablespoon salt. Reduce the heat and simmer until the potatoes are tender when pierced with a fork, 15 to 18 minutes. Drain the potatoes and place them in a large mixing bowl.

Add the mayonnaise, mustard, onions, carrots, and celery to the warm potatoes and, using a spatula, mix well. Add the remaining 1 teaspoon salt, pepper, and parsley and mix well. Sprinkle with the bacon just before serving. Potato salad can be made up to 1 day in advance. Cover and refrigerate, then sprinkle with the bacon just before serving.

tangy coleslaw

Where I come from in North Carolina, you just cannot eat barbecued ribs, pulled pork, or fried chicken without a side of slaw. What really sets this coleslaw apart from all others is the combination of red and green cabbage with the bright flavors of lemon and vinegar.

MAKES 6 TO 8 SERVINGS

1 head green cabbage, finely shredded

½ head red cabbage, finely shredded

2 large carrots, grated

1 medium red onion, quartered and thinly sliced

½ cup sugar

½ cup apple cider vinegar

½ cup mayonnaise

1 tablespoon fresh lemon juice

1 tablespoon kosher salt

1 teaspoon freshly ground black pepper

1 teaspoon celery seeds

1 teaspoon dry mustard

Combine the green cabbage, red cabbage, carrots, and red onion in a large bowl.

Combine the sugar and vinegar in a small saucepan and bring to a simmer over medium heat, stirring until the sugar dissolves. Allow the mixture to cool, then whisk in the mayonnaise, lemon juice, salt, pepper, celery seeds, and mustard.

Pour the dressing over the cabbage and toss to coat before serving.

make it your own

Dress up your slaws with
* broccoli
* grated radishes
* grated cucumbers
* thinly sliced scallions
* chopped pecans
* raisins
* dried cranberries

cobb salad

I love Cobb salad because it includes perfect mini morsels of bacon, avocado, turkey, and crumbled blue cheese—all dressed with a mustardy vinaigrette. Be inspired to present Cobb salad in unique ways. Cut the ingredients into strips and slices, cubes and wedges, and then arrange them in stripes or circles on top of the lettuce. There are no rules, except to make it look as appetizing as possible.

MAKES 6 SERVINGS

DRESSING

2 garlic cloves

⅓ cup red wine vinegar

2 tablespoons Dijon mustard

1½ teaspoons kosher salt

1½ teaspoons freshly ground black pepper

½ cup extra virgin olive oil

SALAD

½ head romaine lettuce, chopped

½ head Boston lettuce, chopped

½ head iceberg lettuce, chopped

1 whole boneless, skinless turkey or chicken breast (about 1½ pounds), cooked and diced

6 bacon slices, cooked (page 137) and crumbled

2 ripe avocados, pitted, peeled, and cut into ½-inch pieces

1 tomato, cored, seeded, and finely diced

½ cup chopped pitted black olives

½ cup crumbled blue cheese

2 hard-boiled eggs, finely chopped

2 tablespoons chopped fresh chives

To make the dressing, put the garlic in a food processor and pulse until finely chopped. Add the vinegar, mustard, salt, and pepper through the feed tube and pulse 3 to 4 times. With the food processor running, add the olive oil in a slow, steady stream, until the dressing is emulsified, 10 to 20 seconds.

To make the salad, combine the lettuces in a large bowl. Pour the dressing over the lettuces and toss well to coat. Arrange the turkey, bacon, avocados, tomato, olives, and blue cheese decoratively over the greens. Sprinkle with the chopped eggs and chives.

sides
=== supporting players ===

TO THIS DAY, the foods I look forward to the most at holiday meals are my mother's side dishes. When we gather for Easter, Thanksgiving, or Christmas dinners, Mom always makes sure that each of her children's favorites fill the table. For my brother, Chip, it's Chunky Sweet Potato Casserole. My sister, Jackie, adores Mom's "Browned" Rice. I can't imagine a holiday table without Mom's mashed potatoes.

These dishes, of course, aren't limited to holidays and special occasions. For busy weeknight dinners, many of them—oven-roasted vegetables, baked beans, and mashed potatoes—taste better when made a day ahead.

Side dishes are those essential supporting players that make the main dish a star attraction.

sautéed green beans

with garlic and bacon

Like many kids, I wasn't too crazy about vegetables. I tried to insist to Mom that pickles were a vegetable, because they started out as cucumbers. For some reason, Mom never bought that line. She soon figured out, however, that by cooking green beans and some other vegetables in bacon drippings and adding some crumbled bacon pieces, I'd happily ask for seconds.

MAKES 6 TO 8 SERVINGS

Kosher salt

2½ pounds green beans, cut into 2-inch pieces

3 tablespoons unsalted butter

8 bacon slices, cooked (page 137) and crumbled; 3 tablespoons drippings reserved

⅔ cup finely chopped scallions

2 garlic cloves, minced

Pinch of cumin

½ teaspoon kosher salt

1 teaspoon freshly ground black pepper

Bring a large pot of salted water to a boil. Add the beans and cook until crisp-tender, about 4 minutes. Drain the beans and rinse them under cold water to cool. Set aside.

Melt the butter with the bacon drippings in a skillet over medium heat. Add the scallions and sauté until tender and beginning to turn golden, about 4 minutes. Add the garlic and sauté for 1 minute more. Add the beans to the skillet and sauté until they are warmed through, about 6 minutes. Sprinkle in the bacon and toss to combine. Season with the cumin, salt, and pepper and transfer to a bowl before serving.

dishin' with DAVID

SAVIN' THE DRIPPINS

Every time Mom fried bacon, she poured any leftover drippings into an old coffee cup that she kept on the back of the stove. She added a spoonful or two of the rendered fat to a skillet whenever she made green beans, lima beans, potatoes, or other vegetables. Don't be so quick to throw out those drippings; they make for great seasoning.

roasted tomatoes
with goat cheese and bread crumbs

What I love about tomatoes is their versatility. While they're best when plucked ripe off the vines during the summer, roasting them brings out their great flavors at any time of year. If you've never tasted roasted tomatoes, you're in for a treat. Here, I scoop out the insides and fill the tomatoes with goat cheese, bread crumbs, and lots of herbs. Once baked, the soft and tender tomatoes become an elegant side dish that deserves to be served with roast chicken, beef tenderloin, or grilled fish.

MAKES 6 SERVINGS

6 beefsteak tomatoes
Vegetable oil spray
2 teaspoons kosher salt
2 teaspoons freshly ground black pepper
½ cup chopped scallions
1 tablespoon minced garlic
1 tablespoon finely chopped fresh basil

1 tablespoon finely chopped fresh rosemary
¼ teaspoon finely chopped fresh thyme
¼ cup extra virgin olive oil
2 tablespoons unsalted butter, at room temperature
2 cups fresh white bread crumbs
4 ounces goat cheese, crumbled

Preheat the oven to 350°F. Spray an 8-inch square baking dish with the vegetable oil spray.

Slice a thin layer off the bottom of each tomato. Stand the tomatoes upright and slice a slightly thicker layer off the tops (reserve the caps). Using a grapefruit spoon or a serrated knife, carefully scoop out the "insides" of the tomatoes and reserve. Sprinkle the insides of the hollowed-out tomatoes with 1 teaspoon of the salt and 1 teaspoon of the pepper.

Combine the scallions, garlic, basil, rosemary, and thyme in a large bowl. Add the olive oil and butter and stir to combine. Add the bread crumbs and toss to coat. Gently stir in the goat cheese.

Divide the bread crumb mixture among the tomato shells, adding enough filling to rise slightly above their tops. Replace the caps on top of the tomatoes. Arrange the tomatoes in the baking dish. Bake for 45 minutes to 1 hour, until they are tender but still hold their shape. Serve immediately.

make it your own

- Bake the bread crumb–goat cheese filling in hollowed-out small zucchini or yellow squash, bell peppers, mushroom caps, or sweet onions.
- Substitute grated Cheddar, mozzarella, or Gruyère for the goat cheese.
- Substitute cooked rice, quinoa, orzo, or couscous for the bread crumbs.

summer squash fritters
with garlic dipping sauce

Just about any vegetable, seafood, or fruit can be dipped into a batter and then deep-fried to make fritters. In late summer, when zucchini and yellow squash are plentiful. I serve these crispy fritters as an appetizer or as a side dish with a super-garlicky dipping sauce. Even though the dip calls for a lot of garlic, once the garlic is roasted, it becomes mild, nutty, and sweet.

MAKES 12 FRITTERS

GARLIC DIPPING SAUCE

2 garlic heads, peeled

Extra virgin olive oil

1 cup mayonnaise

3 tablespoons fresh lemon juice

1 teaspoon kosher salt

¼ teaspoon freshly ground black pepper

¼ cup minced fresh chives

SUMMER SQUASH FRITTERS

1¼ cups all-purpose flour

5 ounces (about ¾ cup) shredded white
    Cheddar

1 teaspoon kosher salt

1 teaspoon freshly ground black pepper

1 teaspoon garlic powder

2 large eggs

1 cup cold beer

1 cup grated zucchini

1 cup grated yellow squash

1 small onion, halved and thinly sliced

½ cup canola oil for frying

To make the dipping sauce, preheat the oven to 375°F.

Put the garlic cloves in a small baking dish and add enough olive oil to cover them completely. Roast until the garlic is soft and golden, about 30 minutes. Remove from the oven and allow the garlic to cool. Strain, but don't discard, the oil from the garlic. Transfer the cooled garlic to a food processor. Add 1 tablespoon of the reserved garlic oil, the mayonnaise, lemon juice, salt, and pepper. Pulse until the mixture is smooth. Transfer the sauce to a bowl and stir in the chives.

To make the fritters, combine the flour, Cheddar, salt, pepper, and garlic powder in a large bowl. In a separate bowl, gently whisk together the eggs and beer. Pour the egg mixture into the flour mixture and stir until combined. Stir in the zucchini, yellow squash, and onion.

Heat the canola oil in a large heavy-bottomed skillet over medium-high heat. Drop about 6 individual tablespoons of batter into the oil and fry until they are golden brown, 2 to 3 minutes per side. Remove the fritters to paper towels to drain. Repeat with the remaining batter. Serve hot with the dipping sauce on the side.

southern fried okra

At every family gathering we went to when I was growing up, there was always a big basket of fried okra on the dinner table to accompany hamburgers, barbecue, or fried fish. In the South, if you have a vegetable garden, you grow okra. It's best in the summer, so if you find a basket at a good price, buy plenty. Then cut up the okra, bread it, and freeze it until you're desperate for a taste of summer during a cold winter.

MAKES 4 TO 6 SERVINGS

1 pound fresh okra

1½ teaspoons kosher salt

1½ cups buttermilk

4 to 6 cups canola oil for frying

1¾ cups cornmeal

3 tablespoons baking powder

Remove the tips and stem ends from the okra. Slice the okra crosswise into ½-inch-thick slices. Transfer the okra to a bowl and sprinkle with ½ teaspoon of the salt. Add the buttermilk and stir to coat. Let the mixture stand for 15 minutes. Drain the okra and discard the buttermilk.

Clip a deep-frying thermometer to the side of a heavy, deep pot. Add the canola oil to the pot and heat until the temperature reaches 375°F on the thermometer.

Mix the cornmeal, baking powder, and the remaining 1 teaspoon salt on a large shallow plate to combine well. Working in batches, dredge the okra slices in the cornmeal and fry until golden brown, 1 to 2 minutes. Transfer the okra to paper towels to drain. Serve hot.

dishin' with DAVID

TRY EVERYTHING, AT LEAST ONCE

Andrew Zimmern, host of *Bizarre Foods*, is known for eating some of the strangest foods all over the world. When we talked one time, Andrew said, "It's just food. If you open yourself up to the world of food, you'll find a lot of things you'll really like. And sometimes some of the goofiest stuff is the tastiest. One man's weird is another man's wonderful." You never know if you like something unless you taste it, so open your mind and your mouth to new flavors and foods.

scrumptious hush puppies

Whenever we visited my grandparents, it was a real treat when they took us out to dinner at a fish camp. A fish camp is what we down South call a seafood restaurant. I can still see the paper-lined red plastic baskets filled with fried fish, some tangy coleslaw in a small cup, and a pile of freshly fried hush puppies. When I make hush puppies, I add corn kernels and Cheddar to the mix. And here's where those bacon drippings (page 96) will come in handy.

MAKES ABOUT 24

1 8.5-ounce box corn muffin mix

1½ cups self-rising flour, plus more if necessary

4 teaspoons sugar

1½ teaspoons kosher salt, or more to taste

1 teaspoon freshly ground black pepper, or more to taste

1½ cups buttermilk

4 bacon slices, cooked (page 137) and finely chopped; ¼ cup bacon drippings reserved

2 large eggs

4 scallions, minced

1 cup frozen corn kernels, thawed

1½ cups (6 ounces) finely shredded Cheddar

Canola oil for frying

Whisk together the muffin mix, flour, sugar, salt, and pepper in a bowl. In a separate bowl, whisk together the buttermilk, bacon, bacon drippings, eggs, and scallions. Stir in the corn. Pour the buttermilk mixture into the corn muffin mixture and stir to combine. Add 1 to 2 tablespoons flour, if necessary, so that the mixture holds together. Stir in the Cheddar. Cover and refrigerate for 30 minutes.

Using a melon baller, shape the batter into 1- to 1½-inch balls.

Clip a deep-frying thermometer to the side of a heavy, deep pot. Add 3 inches of canola oil to the pot and slowly heat the oil to 375°F. Using a slotted spoon, add 6 to 8 hush puppies to the hot oil and fry for 2 minutes, or until golden brown on one side. Turn them and fry for 2 minutes more. (Cook the hush puppies in batches or the oil won't stay hot and they will be soggy rather than crisp.) Using tongs or a slotted spoon, remove the hush puppies to a wire rack or paper towels. Season with salt and pepper to taste. Cook the remaining hush puppies. Serve hot.

vegetable fried rice

I went to college at the University of North Carolina–Chapel Hill, and one summer I worked as a college intern. As a treat, my boss took me to a local restaurant for my first Chinese lunch. I can still remember the beef with broccoli and the fried rice. Boy, was I hooked. When I started cooking, I was determined to learn how to make the rice at home. Fried rice is easy to prepare, but the secret is to use cold, leftover rice. This is also a great way to use up bits and pieces of vegetables—zucchini, peas, carrots, green beans, corn, and broccoli—that may be in your refrigerator.

MAKES 4 TO 6 SERVINGS

½ cup low-sodium soy sauce

1 tablespoon light brown sugar

1 tablespoon rice vinegar

1 tablespoon grated fresh ginger

2 tablespoons canola oil

2 carrots, diced

1 medium onion, diced

1 cup halved sugar snap peas

3 cups cooked cold rice

4 scallions, thinly sliced

2 large eggs, lightly beaten

3 tablespoons dark sesame oil

Whisk together the soy sauce, brown sugar, rice vinegar, and ginger in a small bowl.

Heat the canola oil in a large nonstick skillet over medium-high heat. Add the carrots and onion and cook, stirring occasionally, until the vegetables have softened, 2 to 3 minutes. Add the snap peas and 3 tablespoons of the soy sauce mixture. Cook, stirring, until the snap peas are crisp-tender, 2 to 3 minutes. Transfer the vegetables to a bowl.

Return the skillet to medium heat. Add the rice, scallions, and the remaining soy sauce mixture. Cook until the rice is heated through, 1 to 2 minutes. Push the rice toward the sides of the skillet, leaving a well in the center. Add the eggs to the well and cook, scrambling gently, until they are set. Stir the scrambled eggs into the rice. Stir the vegetables into the rice and drizzle with the sesame oil. Serve hot.

dishin' with DAVID

FROM GOOD TO GRATE

All that mincing garlic, zesting lemons, and shredding cheese takes time and a toll on your fingers and knuckles. I use different sizes of Microplane zesters and graters to make short work of tasks such as grating ginger, garlic, whole spices, chocolate bars, and hard cheeses.

israeli couscous
with peas, asparagus, and mint

This side dish is all about texture, bright flavors, and a burst of citrus. Refreshing and light, it goes with just about anything you put on the grill—chicken, shrimp, fish, steaks, or kebabs. Serve it warm or at room temperature.

MAKES 6 TO 8 SERVINGS

DRESSING

2 tablespoons extra virgin olive oil

2 tablespoons fresh lemon juice

1 garlic clove, minced

½ teaspoon finely grated lemon zest

1 teaspoon kosher salt

½ teaspoon freshly ground black pepper

COUSCOUS

2 tablespoons extra virgin olive oil

1⅓ cups Israeli couscous

1¾ cups water

1 pound thin asparagus, trimmed and diagonally sliced into ¾-inch pieces

½ pound sugar snap peas, trimmed and diagonally sliced into ¾–inch pieces

1 cup frozen peas, thawed

1 garlic clove, minced

⅓ cup chopped fresh mint leaves

½ cup finely grated Parmigiano-Reggiano

To make the dressing, whisk together the olive oil, lemon juice, garlic, lemon zest, salt, and pepper in a small bowl. Set aside.

To make the couscous, heat 1 tablespoon of the olive oil in a saucepan over medium heat. Add the couscous and stir frequently to toast the couscous until brown. Add the water and bring to a boil. Reduce the heat to low, cover the saucepan, and simmer until the liquid is absorbed and the couscous is tender, 5 to 6 minutes. Remove from the heat and let stand.

Heat the remaining 1 tablespoon olive oil in a skillet over medium-high heat. Add the asparagus, snap peas, peas, and garlic. Stir-fry until crisp-tender, 3 to 5 minutes. Transfer the vegetables and couscous to a large bowl. Add the dressing, mint, and Parmesan and toss well before serving.

dishin' with DAVID

KINDS OF COUSCOUS

Most people are familiar with the small-grained semolina couscous from Morocco, but there's also Israeli, or pearl, couscous. Israeli couscous is tiny round balls of wheat, larger than the small-grained couscous from Morocco. Both can be used as a base for vegetables, meat, or just about anything you'd combine with pasta or rice. Look for couscous where rice and other grains are shelved.

make it your own

- Add chopped chives, parsley, basil, or other herbs.
- Add 1 tablespoon Moroccan spice blend, including ground cumin, cinnamon, ginger, clove, and coriander.
- Top with grilled chicken breasts or fish, or a hearty stew.
- Add all kinds of cooked vegetables: carrots, onions, eggplants, zucchini, and tomatoes.
- Toss in a handful of toasted almonds and golden raisins.

mom's "browned" rice

One of Mom's best-loved side dishes is her "browned" rice. You read that right. It's "browned," not brown rice. It's made with beef consommé, which turns the rice brown, and is baked in the oven. To this day, when my family gathers, Mom knows that this side has to be on the menu. It's the perfect accompaniment to roast beef, baked ham, or pork roast.

This dish uses canned consommé, which is beef-based but thicker than stock or broth and gives the rice more flavor.

MAKES 4 SERVINGS

8 tablespoons (1 stick) unsalted butter
1 small onion, finely chopped
1 cup long-grain white rice

2 10.75-ounce cans beef consommé soup
½ cup (2 ounces) shredded Cheddar

Preheat the oven to 350°F.

Melt the butter in a small saucepan. Add the onion and sauté until translucent, about 5 minutes. Set aside.

Combine the rice and consommé in a 3-quart baking dish. Stir in the onion and sprinkle evenly with the Cheddar. Cover the dish with aluminum foil and bake for 50 minutes. Remove the foil and bake for 10 minutes more, or until all the liquid has been absorbed and the top is lightly browned. Serve hot.

make it your own

Add
- dried cranberries
- chopped pecans or almonds
- chopped chives
- sautéed mushrooms
- frozen peas

creamy garlic mashed potatoes

Whenever my mom made Pot Roast with Vegetables (page 185) or Smothered Pork Chops (page 131), we kids knew there would be mashed potatoes as well. I loved to spoon a big pile of mashed potatoes onto my plate, make a well in the center, and fill the "lake" with gravy. These days, when I make mashed potatoes to go with those same comfort classics, I add plenty of garlic. Boiling the garlic with the potatoes mellows the garlic's flavor so it doesn't overpower the dish. Leftover mashed potatoes can be used in endless ways—as the topping on shepherd's pie, as a filling for dumplings, or for frying croquettes.

MAKES 4 SERVINGS

4 medium baking potatoes (about 3 pounds), peeled and quartered

5 large garlic cloves

5 tablespoons unsalted butter

¾ cup half-and-half

¼ cup (2 ounces) sour cream

1 teaspoon kosher salt

¼ teaspoon freshly ground black pepper

Place the potatoes and garlic in a large pot and add enough water to cover. Bring the water to a boil and cook until the potatoes are tender, 15 to 20 minutes.

Drain the potatoes and garlic and return them to the pot. Using a potato masher, mash the potatoes and garlic until no lumps remain. Add the butter and then the half-and-half a little bit at a time, just until the potatoes reach the desired consistency (you may not need all the half-and-half). Add the sour cream, salt, and pepper and stir to combine.

make it your own

- replace half of the white potatoes with an equal amount of sweet potatoes, parsnips, or carrots
- 1 cup cooked and chopped spinach or broccoli
- ½ cup chopped fresh parsley, dill, chives, or rosemary
- 1 to 2 tablespoons Dijon mustard
- 1 cup grated Gouda, Parmigiano-Reggiano, blue cheese, or Cheddar
- sautéed mushrooms
- caramelized onions
- olive oil instead of butter
- 2 tablespoons prepared horseradish
- ¼ cup pesto

over-the-top
twice-baked potatoes

While I usually serve these rich and satisfying treats at dinner parties when roast beef, pork roast, or steaks are the centerpiece, I also offer them up as a main course with a salad or green vegetable for a midweek dinner.

MAKES 4 SERVINGS

4 large baking potatoes

6 bacon slices, chopped into 1-inch pieces

⅓ cup diced green bell pepper

1 jalapeño, stemmed, seeded, and minced

6 smoked bacon slices, cooked (page 137) and crumbled

4 ounces (½ cup) cream cheese, at room temperature

6 ounces sour cream

½ cup heavy cream

¾ cup chopped scallions, plus 2 tablespoons for garnish

¾ cup (3 ounces) shredded Cheddar

¼ cup (1 ounce) freshly grated Parmigiano-Reggiano, plus 2 tablespoons for garnish

1½ teaspoons kosher salt

¾ teaspoon freshly ground black pepper

Paprika (optional)

Preheat the oven to 350°F.

Scrub the potatoes with a vegetable brush and pierce each one several times with a fork. Bake until the skins are crisp and a knife goes easily through the flesh, about 1 hour. Leave the oven on.

Cook the raw bacon in a skillet over medium heat until done, 3 to 4 minutes. Add the bell pepper and jalapeño and sauté until softened, about 5 minutes. Stir in the crumbled bacon and cook for 1 minute. Remove the pan from the heat and allow the mixture to cool slightly.

Combine the cream cheese and sour cream in a large bowl and mix well. Set aside.

Slice the top third lengthwise off each potato. Scoop out most of the flesh, leaving just enough on the bottom and sides for the potatoes to retain their shape. Set aside. Discard the tops.

Transfer the scooped-out potato flesh to the bowl with the cream cheese mixture. Add the cream, scallions, the reserved pepper-bacon mixture, the Cheddar, and Parmigiano-Reggiano and mash well. Season with the salt and pepper.

Fill the reserved potato skins with the potato mixture, mounding it over the top. Bake on a baking sheet until the potatoes are heated through, about 25 minutes. Sprinkle the potatoes with paprika (if using), scallions, and Parmigiano-Reggiano before serving.

natural-cut fresh fries
with sea salt

Yes, that's right. *Fresh* fries, not French fries. No one loves French fries more than I do, but making great French fries requires soaking, rinsing, frying, and then frying them again. Who has that kind of time or patience? I found a way to make fabulous crispy-on-the-outside, tender-on-the-inside fries in the oven. These are so easy too, without the fuss or the mess.

MAKES 4 SERVINGS

2 large baking potatoes, peeled

2 tablespoons extra virgin olive oil

1½ tablespoons plus 1 teaspoon sea salt

Preheat the oven to 425°F.

Bring a large pot of water to a boil. Add the potatoes and cook until they are slightly tender, but not cooked through, 5 to 8 minutes. Drain the potatoes and cut them into equal-size wedges.

Transfer the potato wedges to a colander and toss them with the olive oil and 1½ tablespoons salt. Arrange the potato wedges in a single layer on a large nonstick baking sheet and bake until the bottoms are browned and crisp, about 20 minutes.

Remove the potatoes from the oven and toss with the remaining salt before serving.

beer-battered onion rings
with horseradish-dill dipping sauce

Whenever my family and I went out to eat, I ordered onion rings. I had a very specific way of eating them. When I bit into a big crusty ring and the crunchy coating separated from the sweet onion, I had two treats to dip into ketchup!

What a lot of people don't know is how easy it is to make onion rings at home. The key is to start with quality onions like Vidalias or Walla Wallas, which are available throughout the summer. I like my fried onion rings crisp and puffy, so I add beer. The bubbles make the batter light and fluffy.

MAKES 4 SERVINGS

DIPPING SAUCE

1 cup mayonnaise

¼ cup ketchup

2 tablespoons prepared horseradish

¼ teaspoon paprika

1 teaspoon chopped fresh dill

ONION RINGS

Canola oil for frying

2 cups all-purpose flour

1 large egg, lightly beaten

2 teaspoons garlic powder

2 teaspoons dried oregano

⅛ teaspoon cayenne

1 teaspoon kosher salt

½ teaspoon freshly ground black pepper

1 12-ounce bottle beer

3 large onions, preferably Vidalia, sliced
    into ¼-inch-thick rings and separated

To make the dipping sauce, whisk together the mayonnaise, ketchup, horseradish, paprika, and dill in a small bowl. Set aside while cooking the onion rings.

To make the onion rings, clip a deep-frying thermometer to the side of a heavy, deep pot. Add 2 inches of canola oil to the pot and slowly heat the oil to 350°F. While the oil is heating, whisk together the flour, egg, garlic powder, oregano, cayenne, salt, and black pepper in a bowl. Gradually whisk in the beer, stirring until a thick batter forms.

Dredge the onion slices in the batter. Using tongs, add 4 or 5 onion rings to the hot oil and fry for 1 to 2 minutes, until golden brown. Turn them halfway through cooking. (Cook the onion rings in batches or the oil won't stay hot and the onion rings will be soggy rather than crisp.) Again, using tongs, remove the fried onions to a wire rack or paper towels to drain. Cook the remaining batter-dipped onion rings. Serve hot with the dipping sauce.

sweet potato–pineapple casserole

Mom always made this side dish for holiday dinners—at Easter and Christmas with ham or at Thanksgiving with turkey. I love the tender sweets topped with crushed pineapple and lots of warm spices. When I smell this baking in the oven, it says home and comfort to me.

MAKES 8 TO 10 SERVINGS

Vegetable oil spray

SWEET POTATOES

16 medium sweet potatoes, peeled and quartered

2 8-ounce cans crushed pineapple, liquid drained and saved for another use

1½ cups sugar

6 tablespoons unsalted butter, melted

2 teaspoons kosher salt

2 teaspoons ground cinnamon

¼ teaspoon ground allspice

¼ teaspoon ground nutmeg

4 large eggs

TOPPING

1 cup pecans or walnuts, chopped

½ cup packed dark brown sugar

⅓ cup all-purpose flour

2 tablespoons unsalted butter, melted

To make the potatoes, preheat the oven to 350°F. Spray a 9 x13-inch baking dish with the vegetable oil spray and set aside.

Place the potatoes in a large pot and add enough cold water to cover them completely. Bring the water to a boil and cook until the potatoes are fork-tender, about 40 minutes. Drain and peel the potatoes, then mash them in a large bowl. There should be about 10 cups.

Add the pineapple, sugar, butter, salt, cinnamon, allspice, and nutmeg and beat with an electric mixer until well combined. Beat in the eggs, one at a time. Pour the potato mixture into the prepared baking dish.

To make the topping, mix together the pecans, brown sugar, flour, and butter in a small bowl. Sprinkle the mixture evenly over the sweet potatoes.

Bake the casserole for 30 to 40 minutes, until hot and bubbly and the topping is golden brown. Serve immediately.

potato pancakes

Potato pancakes are traditionally served at holiday meals, but I find that they're also a great breakfast or brunch side dish. The secret to potato pancakes is to squeeze as much water as possible from the grated potatoes so they get nice and crisp in the pan. Serve potato pancakes with simply prepared egg dishes, roast chicken, or grilled steaks and let them be the star of the meal.

MAKES 8 TO 10 PANCAKES

2 large eggs

½ cup grated onion

4 scallions, finely chopped

1 teaspoon kosher salt, plus more to taste

½ teaspoon freshly ground black pepper, plus more to taste

2 pounds baking or Yukon Gold potatoes, peeled

4 tablespoons all-purpose flour

Canola oil for frying

Whisk together the eggs, onion, scallions, salt, and pepper in a bowl. Set aside.

Coarsely grate the potatoes on the large holes of a box grater. Put the grated potatoes in a clean dish towel or cheesecloth and wring out any excess moisture. Add the potatoes and flour to the egg mixture. Stir well to combine.

Heat 1 inch of the canola oil in a large skillet over medium-high heat. Scoop ¼ cup of the potato mixture and, using your hands, shape into a pancake. Fry until the bottoms are golden brown, 6 to 8 minutes. Flip the pancakes and cook on the other side, 4 to 5 minutes more. Transfer the pancakes to a paper towel–lined plate to drain and season immediately with salt and pepper. Transfer the pancakes to a baking sheet lined with paper towels to drain while cooking the remaining pancakes. Serve hot.

make it your own

- Add grated zucchini or carrots to the potato mixture before frying.
- For an elegant appetizer, make silver-dollar-size potato pancakes: Top them with
  - a sliver of smoked salmon and a dollop of sour cream or yogurt
  - a teaspoon of fruit chutney or preserves
  - pickled jalapeños
  - salsa
  - blue cheese and walnuts

oven-roasted vegetables

We don't usually think of vegetables as being sweet, but once they are roasted, their natural sugars become caramelized. They become crisp and rich with just a hint of sweetness. A platter of mixed vegetables will look beautiful on your holiday dinner table, or roast just one kind to accompany a weeknight meal. Beware: Even the kids will like vegetables cooked this way.

MAKES 6 TO 8 SERVINGS

2 medium sweet potatoes, peeled and cut into 1-inch cubes

2 large carrots, cut crosswise into ¾-inch slices

2 medium parsnips, cut into 1-inch slices

1 medium onion, quartered and cut through the root into 1-inch slices

1 turnip, cut into 1-inch cubes

2 small zucchini, cut into 1-inch half moons

3 garlic cloves, coarsely chopped

3 tablespoons extra virgin olive oil

1 tablespoon balsamic vinegar

1 tablespoon chopped fresh rosemary

1 tablespoon chopped fresh thyme

1½ teaspoons kosher salt

2 tablespoons minced fresh parsley

2 tablespoons freshly grated Parmigiano-Reggiano

Preheat the oven to 450°F. Line a baking sheet with aluminum foil.

Combine the sweet potatoes, carrots, parsnips, onion, turnip, zucchini, and garlic in a large bowl. Drizzle with the olive oil and vinegar. Add the rosemary, thyme, and salt. Toss well to combine.

Spread the vegetables onto the prepared baking sheet in a single layer. Roast the vegetables for 50 minutes, or until the vegetables are browned and crisp-tender. Give the pan a good shake once or twice while baking so the vegetables cook evenly. Transfer to a serving platter. Sprinkle the vegetables with the parsley and Parmesan before serving hot or at room temperature.

make it your own

- Use this method with cut-up asparagus, beets, bell peppers, broccoli, cauliflower, fennel, garlic, leeks, mushrooms, shallots, and winter squash.
- Toss the vegetables with your favorite spice mix or rub.
- Roast fruit, such as figs, plums, nectarines, peaches, and grapes, tossed with a bit of brown sugar—great with some vanilla ice cream.

baked corn casserole

When I was working in local television news in Altoona, Pennsylvania, my dear friend Karen often invited me to join her family for a home-cooked meal. One time she served this creamy, sweet casserole with its crusty top. I thought, "This is heaven on a plate!" I have been making it ever since, and when guests enjoy this rich dish at my house, they won't leave without the recipe.

MAKES 6 SERVINGS

Vegetable oil spray
1 8.5-ounce box corn muffin mix
1 14-ounce can creamed corn
1 pound frozen corn kernels, thawed and
    drained

8 tablespoons (1 stick) unsalted butter,
    melted
1 cup (8 ounces) sour cream
1 large egg

Preheat the oven to 350°F. Spray a shallow 3-quart baking dish with the vegetable oil spray.

    Stir together the muffin mix, creamed corn, corn kernels, butter, sour cream, and egg in a large bowl. Mix well, but don't overmix. Pour the batter into the prepared dish. Cover with aluminum foil and bake for 55 to 60 minutes. Remove the foil and bake for 10 minutes more, or until the top is crusty and golden brown. Serve hot.

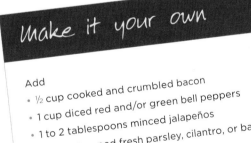

make it your own

Add
- ½ cup cooked and crumbled bacon
- 1 cup diced red and/or green bell peppers
- 1 to 2 tablespoons minced jalapeños
- ½ cup chopped fresh parsley, cilantro, or basil
- 1 cup (4 ounces) shredded Cheddar
- 1 cup crumbled goat cheese
- 1 cup sautéed chopped onions

new england baked beans

Baked beans remain a traditional dish served in homes and restaurants throughout the Northeast. Some people make theirs with maple syrup or molasses, but I use a combination of both. Beans were once cooked for hours in special earthenware bean pots in the embers of a fireplace. I make mine low and slow in my oven and serve them with grilled sausages, burgers, or ribs.

MAKES 8 TO 10 SERVINGS

1 pound dried Great Northern beans
½ pound thickly sliced bacon, chopped
1 Spanish onion, chopped
2 garlic cloves, minced
2 cups ketchup
1 cup Dijon mustard

½ cup apple cider vinegar
1½ cups packed dark brown sugar
⅓ cup molasses
¼ cup maple syrup
¼ cup Worcestershire sauce
½ teaspoon kosher salt

Place the beans in a large pot in water to cover and soak overnight in the refrigerator.

Rinse the beans and pick them over. Place the beans in a Dutch oven and add enough water to cover by 2 inches. Bring the beans to a boil and cook for 2 minutes. Remove the pot from the heat, cover, and let stand for 1 hour.

Drain and rinse the beans. Return the beans to the Dutch oven and add 6 cups water. Bring to a boil, then reduce the heat to a simmer. Cover and cook, until the beans are almost tender, about 2 hours.

Cook the bacon in a skillet over medium heat until crisp. Using tongs, remove the bacon to paper towels to drain. Discard all but 2 tablespoons drippings from the pan. Add the onion to the pan with the drippings and sauté for 3 to 4 minutes, until soft. Add the garlic and cook for 1 minute more. Stir in the ketchup, mustard, vinegar, brown sugar, molasses, maple syrup, Worcestershire sauce, and salt.

Preheat the oven to 275°F.

Drain the beans, reserving the cooking liquid. Put the beans in a 4-quart ovenproof Dutch oven or baking dish. Stir in the bacon and the onion mixture. Cover and bake for 3 hours, stirring every 30 minutes, until the beans are creamy. If the beans seem dry, add reserved cooking liquid as necessary. Serve hot.

easy oven polenta

"Polenta" is a fancy Italian word for "grits" or "cornmeal." The traditional way of making polenta calls for constant stirring for twenty to thirty minutes. I don't know about you, but I just don't have that kind of time. Instead I make polenta in the oven—and very little stirring is required. Use fluffy, yellow polenta as a soft bed to accompany pot roast, short ribs, brisket, chicken, or stew.

MAKES 4 SERVINGS

1 cup coarsely ground cornmeal

1 tablespoon kosher salt

1 teaspoon freshly ground black pepper

2 tablespoons unsalted butter, diced

1 cup freshly grated Parmigiano-Reggiano

Preheat the oven to 350°F.

Stir together the cornmeal, 4 cups cold water, the salt, and pepper in a 1½- to 2-quart shallow baking dish. Bake, uncovered, for 35 to 40 minutes. Open the oven door and pull out the rack. Sprinkle the butter pieces across the top and stir in the Parmigiano-Reggiano. Bake for 10 minutes more. Let the polenta sit for 5 minutes before serving.

make it your own

Add
- grated Monterey Jack, or crumbled goat cheese
- sautéed mushrooms
- caramelized onions
- cooked and chopped spinach

Consider polenta to be like oatmeal for breakfast:
Top with
- jam
- chopped nuts
- apple butter
- honey
- maple syrup
- poached eggs

pork
=== the divine swine ===

MY LOVE OF PORK began when I was a little boy. One of the many things that say comfort and home to me is pork. If you watch *In the Kitchen with David,* then you know my love of the divine swine has grown only stronger over the years as I learned to cook. So I just had to include an entire chapter dedicated to my favorite recipes starring this versatile meat: crunchy bacon, tender pork roast, lovely holiday ham, crisp pork chops, pork ribs, and just about every other part of the pig that can be enjoyed.

The layers and layers of flavor that pork adds to your cooking are distinctly unique. And I can find a place for pork in just about every meal of the day. Don't believe me? Keep reading.

blt mini cups

BLTs were a summer lunch staple at our house. My mother had a sunny garden patch right outside our kitchen where she planted three tomato seedlings every spring. She picked the tomatoes when they were just shy of ripe and let them finish maturing on the windowsill. Slices of warm homegrown tomatoes, crisp bacon slices, and a few lettuce leaves between two slices of mayonnaise-smeared bread is still one of my favorite sandwiches.

I was determined to create a BLT appetizer with those same memorable ingredients. One of bacon's many wonders is that it can be molded into all kinds of shapes. Here it is cut into pieces to fit mini muffin cups. When turned out, the bacon cups hold their shape. These one-bite BLTs are a new twist on a classic. Allow yourself extra time to get the technique just right.

MAKES 12 CUPS

Vegetable oil spray

6 thin bacon slices, cut in half

½ cup mayonnaise

1 teaspoon fresh lemon juice

1 teaspoon freshly ground black pepper

1 pint cherry tomatoes, cut into small dice

1 celery stalk, cut into small dice

3 scallions, cut into small dice

4 or 5 fresh basil leaves, finely chopped

1 teaspoon kosher salt

3 tablespoons unsalted butter, at room temperature

3 slices thin white sandwich bread, toasted, crusts removed, and quartered

Finely chopped fresh parsley

Preheat the oven to 350°F. Invert a 12-cup mini muffin pan on a baking sheet lined with aluminum foil. Lightly spray the inverted muffin cups with the vegetable oil spray.

Wrap half a strip of bacon around the circumference of a muffin cup and bring the "tail" up over the flat top to form a cup. Repeat with the remaining bacon. Spray the insides of a second mini muffin pan and place the pan upside down on top of the first one to hold the bacon cups in place and keep the bacon from shrinking. Don't press the muffin pan. Bake until crisp, about 20 minutes. Remove from the oven and cool for 5 minutes on a wire rack. Remove the top muffin tin, then carefully remove each bacon cup to a paper towel–lined plate.

Whisk together the mayonnaise, lemon juice, and pepper in a bowl. In another bowl, mix together the tomatoes, celery, scallions, basil, and salt. Divide the tomato mixture among the bacon cups. Top with a dollop of the mayonnaise mixture. Lightly butter the toast squares. Place a bacon cup on each square and garnish with parsley before serving.

Make it your own

Fill with a spoonful of
* chicken salad
* baked beans
* mushrooms
* Cheddar
* scrambled eggs
* peanut butter

deviled eggs
with scallions and crispy bacon

I have never been to a summer barbecue, family gathering, or church picnic where platters of deviled eggs weren't on the picnic table. Plain deviled eggs are tasty, but I figured they'd have even more zing if I added two great ingredients—mild scallions and crispy bits of bacon. Bring these to your next occasion and your deviled eggs will never be called ordinary again.

MAKES 24 SERVINGS

12 large eggs, hard boiled (below) and peeled

6 bacon slices, cooked (page 137), and crumbled, with 1 slice reserved for garnish

½ cup mayonnaise

1 scallion, thinly sliced

1½ teaspoons Dijon mustard

1½ teaspoons caper or pickle juice

Kosher salt and freshly ground black pepper

Paprika

Cut each egg in half lengthwise. Scoop out the yolks and place them in a bowl. Mash the yolks with a fork, then stir in the crumbled bacon, mayonnaise, scallion, mustard, and caper juice until well blended. Add salt and pepper to taste.

Spoon, or pipe with a pastry bag fitted with a tip, about 1 tablespoon of the yolk mixture into each egg half. Crumble the remaining piece of cooked bacon. If serving immediately, garnish the egg yolks with the bacon. Or cover and refrigerate for up to 4 hours. Garnish with the bacon and dust with paprika just before serving.

dishin' with DAVID

COME OUT OF YOUR SHELL

Yes, there's a right way and a wrong way to boil eggs. You want hard-boiled eggs that are easy to peel and with their yolks centered in the whites. Start with room-temperature eggs. Put the eggs in a single layer in a saucepan with little room for them to roll around and cover with 1 to 2 inches of cold water. Bring to a boil over medium heat. Stir the eggs with a spoon every once in a while to keep the yolks centered. Once the water comes to a boil, turn off the heat. Leave the eggs in the hot water for 15 to 20 minutes. (The water's residual heat cooks them.) Drain the hot water and cover them with cold water. After a few minutes, drain the water and vigorously twirl the eggs in the saucepan to crack them. Then finish peeling them by hand.

bacon-wrapped poblano peppers

Here's a dish that unquestionably proves my theory that everything is better with bacon. Wrapping poblano peppers with bacon makes all the flavors here really pop and gives the peppers a little crunchy, smoky something extra. Serve this as a side dish with barbecued ribs or grilled sausage.

MAKE 4 SERVINGS

4 large poblano peppers

2 tablespoons unsalted butter

½ medium onion, thinly sliced

1 8-ounce package cream cheese, at room temperature

4 scallions, chopped

1 teaspoon chopped fresh thyme

1 teaspoon ground cinnamon

½ teaspoon sugar

¼ teaspoon kosher salt

⅛ teaspoon freshly ground black pepper

8 bacon slices

Preheat the oven to 425°F.

Cut ¼ inch off the tops of the peppers, keeping the tops and stems to create little "hats." Using a spoon, scrape out the seeds from inside the peppers and their tops and discard the seeds.

Melt the butter in a skillet over medium heat. Add the onion and cook until lightly browned, 8 to 10 minutes.

Combine the cooked onion, cream cheese, scallions, thyme, cinnamon, sugar, salt, and black pepper in a food processor. Blend until smooth.

Stuff each pepper with the filling and put the tops back on. Wrap each pepper with 2 bacon slices, using toothpicks to secure the bacon, if necessary. Arrange the peppers on a wire rack over a shallow baking pan so that the bacon fat drips into the bottom of the pan. Putting the peppers at a 45-degree angle helps to keep the filling inside the peppers. (Crumpled aluminum foil works well.) Bake until the peppers are tender and the cheese is melted, about 30 minutes. Serve hot.

holiday ham
with honey-mustard glaze

At my house, it wouldn't be Christmas, Easter, or any other holiday unless there's a ham at the center of my table. What makes it extra gorgeous and extra flavorful is my glaze of honey, mustard, pineapple juice, and brown sugar. Don't forget to hold on to that ham bone for making White Bean and Ham Soup (page 77).

MAKES 12 TO 14 SERVINGS

1 5- to 7-pound fully cooked, spiral-cut
    unglazed ham

HONEY-MUSTARD GLAZE

⅛ cup honey

¼ cup Dijon mustard

⅛ teaspoon ground cloves

½ cup pineapple juice

½ cup packed brown sugar

Preheat the oven to 325°F.

Place the ham on a rack in a roasting pan. Cover the ham with aluminum foil and bake for 30 minutes to 1 hour. The ham needs to cook for 10 to 12 minutes per pound; 1 hour to 80 minutes.

To make the glaze, combine the honey, mustard, cloves, pineapple juice, and brown sugar in a saucepan over low heat. Cook until the sugar is dissolved, about 10 minutes.

Remove the ham from the oven, discard the foil, and baste with the glaze. Return the ham to the oven and baste every 10 minutes until an instant-read thermometer inserted into the thickest part of the meat registers 140°F. Remove from the oven and let sit for 5 minutes before slicing and serving.

dishin' with DAVID

THE GRAVY TRAIN

I'm a dunker. I dunk my bacon in syrup and my grilled cheese in my tomato soup. And I like to dunk my ham in this glaze, so I sometimes make a double batch. Any that's left over is heated in a saucepan with a few tablespoons of water to thin it out, then passed in a gravy boat at the table.

north carolina barbecued pulled pork sandwiches

I'm a born and bred Tar Heel, a true son of North Carolina. When we Tar Heels talk about barbecue, we mean pork butt rubbed with spices, then *slooooowly* roasted at a low temperature for hours. When the tender meat can be easily pulled apart with just the touch of a fork, it's done. Then, the meat is tossed with a savory, not sweet, vinegary barbecue sauce with a touch of heat. The dressed pork is then piled on a bun and topped with a heaping helping of Tangy Coleslaw (page 91), and extra sauce is passed in squirt bottles at the table.

MAKES 6 TO 8 SERVINGS

RUB

2 teaspoons paprika

2 teaspoons brown sugar

1 teaspoon garlic powder

1 teaspoon onion powder

1 teaspoon dry mustard

½ teaspoon kosher salt

½ teaspoon freshly ground black pepper

4 to 5 pounds pork butt

SAUCE

8 tablespoons (1 stick) unsalted butter

⅓ cup ketchup

3 jalapeños, stemmed, seeded, and chopped

3 tablespoons fresh lemon juice

2 tablespoons honey

2 tablespoons Dijon mustard

2 tablespoons Worcestershire sauce

2 teaspoons chili powder

2 teaspoons kosher salt

1 teaspoon freshly ground black pepper

1 cup apple cider vinegar

¼ cup red wine vinegar

8 hamburger buns

To make the rub, combine the paprika, brown sugar, garlic powder, onion powder, dry mustard, salt, and pepper in a small bowl. Rub the mixture all over the pork butt. Put the pork in a roasting pan. Cover with plastic wrap and refrigerate for at least 2 hours or overnight.

Preheat the oven to 275°F.

Remove the plastic wrap and roast the pork for 5 to 6 hours. The pork is done when it's so tender that it can be easily shredded with a fork.

To make the sauce, combine the butter, ketchup, jalapeños, lemon juice, honey, Dijon mustard, Worcestershire sauce, chili powder, salt, and pepper in a large saucepan over medium heat. Bring to a boil, remove the pan from the heat, whisk in the cider vinegar and red wine vinegar, and set aside to cool.

Once the pork is cooked, remove it from the oven and let sit for 10 minutes. Using two forks, shred the pork into small pieces. Add the meat to the sauce and let sit for 30 minutes to 1 hour to absorb the sauce. Gently reheat the meat and sauce until warm. Serve the shredded pork on the buns and pass extra sauce.

breaded pork cutlets

The first time I had authentic schnitzel was when QVC sent me to Germany for ten days to shop for Oktoberfest collectibles. My co-workers and I traveled through the countryside to visit craftspeople and see their wares. But for me, the highlight of the trip was stopping for lunch every day and enjoying German ultimate comfort food—pork schnitzel. Very thinly pounded pork cutlets were breaded and quickly fried until crisp on the outside, yet tender inside. Probably the most famous version is Wiener schnitzel made with veal. I also make it with chicken or even turkey cutlets. But because we're talking divine swine here, it's the pork version that I prefer. For perfect cutlets every time, the meat is first dipped in flour, then in beaten eggs with buttermilk, then again in flour, followed by a dunk in bread crumbs before it's cooked in a hot skillet with oil. Serve with Skillet Apples with Cranberries (page 235) and some Oven-Roasted Vegetables (page 114).

MAKES 5 OR 6 SERVINGS

1 pound thinly sliced boneless pork loin cutlets

Kosher salt and freshly ground black pepper

1 cup all-purpose flour

1 large egg, lightly beaten

2 tablespoons buttermilk

2 cups panko (Japanese bread crumbs)

¼ cup extra virgin olive oil

2 tablespoons unsalted butter

Lemon wedges

Trim any excess fat from the pork chops. Using a meat mallet, pound each chop to a ⅛- to ¼-inch thickness. Season the cutlets with salt and pepper.

Spread the flour in a shallow dish. In a second dish, combine the egg and buttermilk. Spread the panko in a third dish. Dredge the cutlets in the flour, then in the egg mixture, then in the panko.

Heat the olive oil and butter in a large skillet over medium heat. Add the cutlets and fry until golden brown and cooked through, 2 to 2½ minutes per side. Serve with lemon wedges.

smothered pork chops

When I was in college at UNC, and my friends and I were longing for a taste of home and our mothers' cooking, we'd head over to the K&W Cafeteria. For me, there was one dish in particular that I really missed: smothered pork chops. The ladies behind the counter knew us by our first names and became like family to us, cooking all our favorite Southern dishes. They'd say, "David, darlin' what can I get you today?" I always answered, "Smothered pork chops, please." The thick pork chops were panfried and simmered with lots and lots of onions and pan gravy. And I always ordered biscuits so I wouldn't miss one drop of the spectacular gravy. Here's how I make smothered pork chops, always remembering those kind, wonderful ladies at K&W when I do.

MAKES 4 SERVINGS

1½ teaspoons kosher salt

1½ teaspoons garlic powder

½ teaspoon freshly ground black pepper

½ teaspoon paprika

¼ teaspoon ground coriander

¼ teaspoon ground sage

4 pork chops (preferably bone in), ¾ to 1 inch thick

½ cup all-purpose flour

½ cup canola oil

1 sweet onion, such as Vidalia, julienned

2 cups low-sodium chicken broth

1 fresh rosemary sprig

Combine the salt, garlic powder, pepper, paprika, coriander, and sage in a small bowl. Rub about ¾ teaspoon of the seasoning over each pork chop. (Reserve the remaining seasoning for the onion gravy.) Spread ¼ cup of the flour in a shallow dish. Dredge each pork chop in the flour.

Heat the canola oil in a heavy skillet over medium-high heat. Add the pork chops and cook until they are well browned, about 3 minutes per side. Transfer the pork chops to a paper towel–lined plate to drain.

Add the onion to the skillet (do not pour off any drippings). Cook until the onion is softened and beginning to brown, 7 to 8 minutes Add the remaining ¼ cup flour and cook, whisking constantly, until the mixture is thickened and golden brown. (If the mixture seems too thick, add a few teaspoons of water.) Add the chicken broth and whisk until smooth. Stir in the remaining seasoning. Bring the mixture to a boil over medium-high heat. Return the pork chops to the skillet and add the rosemary. Reduce the heat to a simmer, cover, and cook until the pork is tender, about 1 hour.

mustard-glazed rosemary pork tenderloins

Pork tenderloin for me is like a blank canvas is to an artist. Depending on what spices and herbs I use, I can flavor it in endless ways. But my favorite preparation is to coat the pork with a savory rub of mustard, rosemary, cracked peppercorns, and spices. The mustard and peppercorns give the meat just the right amount of bite while the rosemary and thyme add fragrance and flavor.

MAKES 4 TO 6 SERVINGS

2 tablespoons honey

2 tablespoons extra virgin olive oil

2 tablespoons coarse-grain mustard

1 tablespoon Dijon mustard

2 tablespoons fresh lemon juice

1 teaspoon minced garlic

Chopped fresh rosemary leaves from 2
    4-inch sprigs

1 teaspoon fresh thyme leaves

1½ teaspoons kosher salt

1 tablespoon coarsely ground black
    pepper

2 1-pound pork tenderloins, trimmed and
    silver skin removed

Whisk together the honey, olive oil, coarse mustard, Dijon mustard, lemon juice, garlic, rosemary, thyme, salt, and pepper in a shallow dish large enough to hold the pork tenderloins. Add the tenderloins, turn to coat, and marinate in the refrigerator for at least 1 hour or overnight.

Preheat the oven to 425°F.

Heat a large ovenproof skillet over medium-high heat. Add the tenderloins and brown on all sides. Transfer the skillet to the oven and cook the pork for 15 to 18 minutes, until the temperature on an instant-read thermometer reads 165°F. Let the tenderloins rest on a cutting board for 5 minutes. Cut on the diagonal into thin slices and serve.

pork pot roast

When you mention pot roast to most people, they usually think of a dish made with beef. But my mother's pork version is one of my more memorable comfort foods. Her pork pot roast is cooked low and slow for hours in a slow cooker until it's fork-tender. This remains my sister's favorite meal when we all get together. The thick gravy is so good that I almost forget my table manners and want to lick the bowl. Instead, I make sure there are plenty of warm biscuits to sop up every drop.

MAKES 8 SERVINGS

1 3- to 4-pound boneless bottom round pork roast
½ cup all-purpose flour
Kosher salt and freshly ground black pepper
¼ cup canola oil
2 onions, quartered
3 garlic cloves, smashed

1 tablespoon tomato paste
1 cup dry red wine
3 cups beef stock
2 fresh thyme sprigs
2 bay leaves
3 carrots, sliced into ½-inch pieces
6 red potatoes, quartered
Freshly chopped parsley

Preheat the oven to 300°F.

Dry the roast with paper towels. Dredge the roast with the flour and season on all sides with salt and pepper. Heat the canola oil in a Dutch oven over medium-high heat and sear the roast on all sides. Transfer the roast to a plate.

Add the onions, garlic, and tomato paste to the pot and cook for 3 to 5 minutes. Add the red wine, stirring to scrape up any browned bits from the bottom of the pot. Cook and reduce to ½ cup. Return the roast to the pot and add the beef stock, thyme, and bay leaves. Bring the liquid to a simmer, cover, and place in the oven.

Roast for 2½ hours and then add the carrots and potatoes. Continue to cook for 2 more hours. Transfer the roast to a cutting board and let rest for 15 to 20 minutes. Slice and place on a serving platter. Skim the fat off the braising liquid and serve the sauce with the roast. Garnish with the parsley.

smoked gouda–bacon cheeseburgers

Foodies, when making cheeseburgers, add a double dose of smoky flavor with smoked Gouda and strips of bacon. These burgers are a great year-round treat because you can make them on your outdoor grill when the weather is warm or in a grill pan on your cooktop. How can you beat a grilled burger punched up with smoked bacon and smoked Gouda on a toasted bun?

MAKES 4

5 bacon slices, diced
1 large onion, chopped
1 cup fresh spinach leaves
2 garlic cloves
1 large egg
1 teaspoon liquid smoke
1 teaspoon kosher salt

½ teaspoon freshly ground black pepper
¼ teaspoon cayenne
1 pound ground chuck
1 4-ounce piece smoked Gouda, cut into 4 cubes
4 hamburger buns, toasted

Preheat an outdoor grill (if using).

Place the bacon in a large skillet and cook over medium heat. Fry, stirring occasionally. When the bacon is almost done, add the onion and spinach. Cook until the bacon is crisp, the onion is tender, and the spinach is wilted. Add the garlic and cook for 1 minute. Using a slotted spoon, remove the bacon mixture from the skillet and transfer to a food processor. Pulse 3 to 4 times to chop finely. Do not puree.

Whisk together the egg, liquid smoke, salt, black pepper, and cayenne in a large bowl. Add the bacon mixture and ground chuck. Using your hands, thoroughly mix the burger mixture and then shape it into 4 patties.

Poke 1 cheese cube into the center of each burger. Place the patties on the grill or grill pan over medium heat and cook for 5 to 7 minutes per side, or until desired doneness. Serve on buns.

dishin' with DAVID

MAKIN' BACON

How to describe bacon? Let me count the ways. Salty and savory. Crispy and crunchy. Sizzling and smoky. Pure deliciousness no matter how you say it. I have several favorite ways for makin' bacon, depending on how much I need for a recipe. Whichever one you choose, always remove the bacon from the fridge and let it sit at room temperature for a good 20 to 30 minutes before cooking.

Panfry: Put the bacon slices in a cold, not preheated, skillet so they cook evenly. Let the bacon cook over medium heat for 3 minutes on one side. Avoid the temptation to flip it back and forth. When one side is to your liking, turn the bacon and cook until desired crispiness. Remove the cooked bacon to paper towels to drain for a minute or two before serving. If chopping or crumbling up the bacon to use in other dishes, wait until the slices are cool enough to handle.

Microwave: For crisp bacon, place 2 layers of paper towels on a microwave-safe plate. Arrange 4 to 6 slices of bacon—don't overlap them—on top, then cover with another paper towel. Microwave on high for 3 minutes, then check for doneness. Microwave for 2 minutes more.

Oven fry: When I need a big batch of bacon for brunches or holiday meals, I turn to this method that restaurant pros use. And bacon cooked this way doesn't get all curly! Line a baking sheet with aluminum foil for easy cleanup. Arrange the bacon on the baking sheet—no overlapping allowed. Put the baking sheet in the oven. Turn on the oven to 400°F—no preheating; always start your bacon at room temperature for even cooking—and bake for 10 to 15 minutes.

crispy, cheesy
hash brown casserole
with bacon

I spend a lot of time on the Delaware shore during the summer months. There's a restaurant there that serves a side dish of hash browns with cheese. Although I always order it, I was inspired to go home and put my own spin on it. And that spin is—you guessed it—a generous amount of bacon and extra cheese. Serve this savory side at breakfast, lunch, or dinner.

MAKES 10 TO 12 SERVINGS

Vegetable oil spray
1 30-ounce package frozen hash brown
    potatoes, thawed
1 10.75-ounces can cream of celery soup
1 10.75-ounce can cream of chicken soup
1 cup (8 ounces) sour cream
6 bacon slices, cooked (page 137) and
    crumbled

10 tablespoons unsalted butter, melted
1 cup (6 ounces) plus 1 cup (6 ounces)
    shredded extra sharp Cheddar
½ cup minced scallions (white and light
    green parts)
½ teaspoon kosher salt
½ teaspoon freshly ground black pepper
¾ cup fresh bread crumbs

Preheat the oven to 350°F. Spray a 2- to 2½-quart baking dish with the vegetable oil spray.

Combine the potatoes, cream of celery soup, cream of chicken soup, sour cream, bacon, ½ cup of the melted butter, 1½ cups of the Cheddar, the scallions, salt, and pepper in a large bowl and mix well. Spread the potato mixture in the prepared baking dish.

Combine the bread crumbs with the remaining 2 tablespoons melted butter in a small bowl. Sprinkle the remaining 2 cups Cheddar over the surface of the potatoes, then top with the bread crumb mixture. Bake the casserole for 25 to 35 minutes, until hot and lightly browned.

roasted vidalia onions stuffed
with bacon and cheese

One of the lovely luxuries of summertime is the abundant harvest of sweet Vidalia onions. True Vidalia onions are grown only in and around Vidalia, Georgia, about two hundred miles west of Savannah. They're called "sweet" onions because they're not as pungent as varieties grown elsewhere and won't make you cry—unless they're tears of joy because Vidalias are so good. Since Vidalias are nice and big—some as big as softballs—I hollow them out, bake them until tender, and then fill them with bacon and three kinds of cheese. Then I pop them under the broiler just until the cheeses bubble. Serve the onions warm and start collecting all the compliments.

MAKES 6 SERVINGS

6 Vidalia onions

¼ cup extra virgin olive oil

1 teaspoon kosher salt

1 teaspoon freshly ground black pepper

4 bacon slices, cooked, but not too crisp
    (page 137), and chopped

1 tablespoon chopped fresh basil

1 tablespoon chopped fresh parsley

1 teaspoon brown sugar

¼ cup (1 ounce) shredded mozzarella

¼ cup (1 ounce) shredded provolone

¼ cup (1 ounce) freshly grated
    Parmigiano-Reggiano

Preheat the oven to 350°F.

Cut a thin slice from the top and bottom of each onion. Peel off the dry outer skin of the onion. Using a paring knife or melon baller, hollow out a 1- to 1½-inch cavity in the center of each onion.

Brush each cavity with the olive oil, then season with the salt and pepper. Stand the onions upright in a baking dish large enough to hold them in a single layer. Bake, uncovered, for 1½ to 2 hours, until the onions are brown and tender. Remove the onions and turn on the broiler.

Combine the bacon, basil, parsley, brown sugar, mozzarella, provolone, and Parmigiano-Reggiano in a bowl. Fill the cavities of the baked onions with the cheese mixture; they should overflow. Put the dish under the broiler and broil until the cheese mixture melts, 3 to 5 minutes. Serve hot.

casseroles
and one-pot meals
=== dinner in one dish ===

WHEN MOM PULLED a hot casserole out of the oven, my brother, sister, and I could barely wait until she piled our plates with mac 'n' cheese, cheeseburger casserole, or lasagne. For busy people like Mom, casseroles and one-pot meals are low-maintenance lifesavers when it comes to getting dinner on the table.

These recipes are exceptionally versatile. No shrimp in the house for jambalaya? Use chicken or turkey instead. No pepperoni for the Pepperoni Pizza Pasta Bake? Substitute your favorite pizza toppings, such as mushrooms or peppers. Out of ground turkey for the shepherd's pie? Try the dish with ground beef or the traditional way with ground lamb.

Every one of these dishes can be made ahead, refrigerated overnight, and then popped into the oven when you walk in the door. In fact, some of them—especially the chili—taste even better when reheated the next day. With fewer dishes to wash, casseroles and one-dish dinners make for easy cleanup.

To me, what's comfort food unless you can share it with others? While these dishes make me happy and satisfied, they make me even happier when I can share them with friends and family. Bring one of these American classics to your next potluck dinner, girls' nights, or family reunions. And share the love.

═ my ultimate macaroni and cheese ═

I've often been asked about my all-time favorite food. That's easy. Without a doubt and hands down, it's macaroni and cheese. There's nothing like the aroma that fills the kitchen when this dish is bubbling in the oven. My recipe calls for five different cheeses and even includes some smoky bacon to give it an extra layer of flavor.

MAKES 6 SERVINGS

1 tablespoon plus 1 teaspoon kosher salt

¾ pound cavatappi, rotini, or fusilli

3 cups half-and-half

2 large eggs

1½ cups (6 ounces) shredded extra sharp
  Cheddar

1 cup (4 ounces) shredded mozzarella

1 cup (4 ounces) shredded Monterey Jack

8 ounces Velveeta, cubed

¼ cup (1 ounce) freshly grated
  Parmigiano-Reggiano

1 cup milk

2 teaspoons dry mustard

1 teaspoon garlic powder

1 teaspoon onion powder

½ teaspoon paprika

1 teaspoon freshly ground black pepper

6 bacon slices, cooked (page 137) and
  crumbled

Preheat the oven to 350°F.

Bring a large pot of water to a boil. Add 1 tablespoon of the salt and the pasta and cook until tender but still firm to the bite, 8 to 10 minutes. Drain the pasta in a colander and set aside.

While the pasta is cooking, heat the half-and-half in a large saucepan over medium heat. Just before the mixture starts to boil, remove the pan from the heat and let cool for 5 minutes.

Whisk the eggs in a bowl, then whisk in 2 cups of the warm half-and-half. (This will keep the eggs from scrambling.) Pour the egg mixture into the saucepan and whisk to combine.

Stir 1 cup of the Cheddar, all the mozzarella, Monterey Jack, Velveeta, and Parmigiano-Reggiano, and the milk into the saucepan. Heat the saucepan on medium-low heat to help melt the cheese. Whisk in the mustard, garlic powder, onion powder, paprika, the remaining 1 teaspoon salt, and the pepper. Do not let the mixture boil.

Toss the cooked pasta and cheese sauce together and then pour into a 4-quart baking dish. Top with the remaining ½ cup Cheddar. Bake for 20 minutes. Sprinkle an even layer of crumbled bacon on top and bake for 10 minutes more.

dishin' with DAVID

WHAT'S IN A NAME?

Don't you just love the names of all those pasta shapes? *Orecchiette* means "little ears." *Farfalle* translates as "butterflies." *Rotini* are "spirals." You can use any short, twisted pasta shape in this recipe, but my favorite is *cavatappi*, which means "corkscrews."

cheesy cheeseburger casserole

Forgive me for getting a little "cheesy" here, but that's just what this one-dish wonder is all about: cheese. Everything we love about melted cheese—rich, ooey, gooeyness—is right here in this cheeseburger casserole. It's easy to make, can be put together ahead and frozen, and it's kid friendly. For kids of all ages, that is.

MAKES 6 SERVINGS

1 tablespoon plus 1 teaspoon kosher salt

1 16-ounce package elbow macaroni

2 pounds ground beef

1 large onion, chopped

2 8-ounce cans tomato sauce

⅛ teaspoon freshly ground black pepper

1 cup (8 ounces) ricotta cheese

¼ cup (2 ounces) sour cream

⅓ cup chopped green bell pepper

⅓ cup chopped scallions

½ cup (2 ounces) shredded Cheddar

¼ cup (1 ounce) shredded mozzarella

¼ cup chopped fresh parsley

Preheat the oven to 350°F.

Bring a large pot of water to a boil. Add 1 tablespoon of the salt and the macaroni and cook until tender but still firm to the bite, 7 to 8 minutes. Drain well.

Heat a large skillet over medium-high heat. Add the beef and onion and cook, stirring, until the beef is well browned. Carefully drain the fat from the skillet and stir in the tomato sauce, the remaining 1 teaspoon salt, and pepper. Bring to a simmer over low heat while preparing the remaining ingredients.

Combine the ricotta, sour cream, bell pepper, and scallions in a medium bowl. Spread half of the pasta in the bottom of a 9 x 13-inch baking dish. Top with the ricotta mixture, then the remaining pasta. Pour the meat mixture over the top. Sprinkle with the Cheddar and mozzarella. Bake the casserole until the cheese is melted and lightly browned, about 20 minutes. Sprinkle with the parsley before serving.

dishin' with DAVID — LET THEM BE—FOR TEN MINUTES

Recipes often tell us to let the meat or casserole "rest" for ten minutes before carving or serving them. If you cut into the cheeseburger—or any—casserole when it comes right out of the oven, the pieces will be runny and won't hold together. By allowing casseroles to sit for a bit and reabsorb some of the melted cheeses and liquid ingredients, the food will hold together for easier serving.

And those casseroles are hot. Too hot to eat when they come right out of the oven. So let them be for ten minutes before digging in.

shrimp and sausage jambalaya

Jambalaya is a Creole classic from southern Louisiana. Unlike in gumbo, a stew served on a scoop of white rice, the rice in jambalaya is cooked with all the other ingredients for a hearty one-pot dish that is both forgiving and versatile. Change up the shrimp with chicken or another seafood. Add more—or less—sausage and ham. It's up to you. Did anyone say Mardi Gras? Where are my beads?

MAKES 6 SERVINGS

2 tablespoons extra virgin olive oil

1 pound chorizo sausage, sliced ¼ inch thick

1 pound smoked ham, cut into ½-inch cubes

1 tablespoon unsalted butter

1 large onion, diced

2 large celery stalks, diced

1 large green bell pepper, cored, seeded, and diced

1 16-ounce can diced tomatoes with their juices

3 garlic cloves, minced

½ to 1 jalapeño, stemmed, seeded, and minced, or ½ teaspoon cayenne

1 tablespoon tomato paste

2 cups low-sodium chicken stock

1½ cups long-grain white rice, rinsed

1 bay leaf

1 teaspoon kosher salt

1 teaspoon freshly ground black pepper

¼ to ½ teaspoon hot sauce

1 pound medium shrimp (20 to 24 count), peeled and deveined

¾ cup chopped fresh parsley

½ cup chopped scallions

Heat the olive oil in a large pot or Dutch oven over medium heat. Add the chorizo and sauté until well browned, 8 to 10 minutes. Transfer the chorizo to a bowl. Add the ham to the pot and sauté until lightly browned, 8 to 10 minutes. Transfer the ham to the bowl with the chorizo.

Melt the butter in the pot. Add the onion, celery, and bell pepper and sauté until the onion is translucent, 8 to 10 minutes. Add the tomatoes, garlic, jalapeño, and tomato paste and bring to a simmer. Simmer about 10 minutes, until the flavors are blended.

Add the chicken stock and bring the mixture to a rolling boil. Stir in the rice, bay leaf, salt, pepper, and hot sauce. Add the chorizo and ham and bring the mixture to a boil. Reduce the heat and simmer, covered, for 20 minutes.

Add the shrimp and stir to combine. Remove the pot from the heat, cover, and allow the jambalaya to steam until the shrimp are cooked through, about 15 minutes. Garnish with the parsley and scallions before serving.

ultimate game-day chili

Get ten people in a room and when you ask them about their favorite chili, you'll get ten different answers. Chili lovers can discuss for hours whether chili should or shouldn't contain beans. Should the meat be ground up or in chunks? What's the difference between Texas and Cincinnati chili? All this talk takes place because chili is one of America's most beloved comfort foods.

So, let me jump in to the discussion. I worked and reworked my chili recipe, so it tastes like what I had in mind. When it comes to making this satisfying dish, there are a couple of things to remember. Give the chili time and cook it low and slow throughout the day, allowing the aromas to fill your house. Even better, make it the day before and reheat it. Make plenty of chili and freeze it. Use a variety of meats, such as ground turkey or some pork cubes, all in the same batch for layers of flavor and different textures. Serve this on a cold winter's day, after skiing or playing touch football. It's great after watching the Super Bowl or the Final Four, or for no reason at all, other than that you just love it.

MAKES 12 TO 14 SERVINGS

1 to 1½ pounds beef chuck roast, cut into 1-inch cubes

1 pound ground beef

1 pound Italian sausage (mild or hot), casings removed and sausage crumbled

2 teaspoons kosher salt, plus more to taste

Freshly ground black pepper

1 large red onion, chopped

1 large red bell pepper, cored, seeded, and chopped

1 large yellow bell pepper, cored, seeded, and chopped

2 garlic cloves, chopped

1 7-ounce can chipotle peppers in adobo, chopped

1 4-ounce can chopped mild green chiles

1 14.5-ounce can crushed tomatoes

2 cups beef stock

1 6-ounce can tomato paste

1 12-ounce bottle beer

½ cup chili sauce

1 tablespoon chili powder

1 tablespoon ground cumin

1½ teaspoons cayenne

1 15.5-ounce can red kidney beans, drained and rinsed

1 8-ounce can cannellini beans, drained and rinsed

1 8-ounce can black beans, drained and rinsed

Shredded Cheddar

Sour cream or plain yogurt

Chopped scallions

Combine the beef cubes, ground beef, and crumbled sausage in a large Dutch oven over medium heat. Cook the meats, stirring regularly, until they are evenly browned. Drain the meat, set aside, and discard the drippings from the pan. Season to taste with salt and black pepper.

Add the red onion, red bell pepper, yellow bell pepper, and garlic to the pot. Cook, stirring occasionally, until the vegetables are tender, 5 to 7 minutes.

Stir in the cooked meats, the chipotles and sauce, the green chiles, tomatoes, 1 cup of the beef stock, the tomato paste, beer, chili sauce, chili powder, cumin, cayenne, and the 2 teaspoons salt. Simmer the chili, stirring occasionally, for 1 to 1½ hours. If the chili seems too thick, add the remaining 1 cup beef stock. Add the kidney beans, cannellini beans, and black beans during the last 20 minutes of cooking.

Serve the chili in big bowls and let each person add Cheddar, sour cream, and scallions as desired.

dishin' with DAVID

CHILLY OUTSIDE, CHILI INSIDE

No matter what kind of meats—beef, turkey, chicken, sausage, or a combination—you're using, always brown them first to lock in their flavors before adding liquids or any other ingredients to the pot.

- Cook the chili the day before you plan to serve it. Let it cool, then cover and refrigerate overnight to give all the flavors time to blend. Or, prepare the chili in the morning and let it simmer all day until serving time.
- I like my chili with a good dose of heat, but if you don't, use mild sausage instead of hot and omit the chipotle peppers in adobo and the cayenne.

pepperoni pizza pasta bake

I've loved pepperoni pizza ever since I was old enough to order my first hot, gooey slice. One day I wondered what would happen if I combined my favorite pizza toppings in a baked pasta dish. Violà! Don't care for pepperoni? Then add your own preferred toppings. Serve a simple green salad and some garlic bread for a winning meal the entire family will love.

MAKES 4 SERVINGS

Vegetable cooking spray

1 tablespoon kosher salt

1 12-ounce box penne or ziti

½ pound mild Italian sausage, casings removed and sausage crumbled

½ cup chopped onion

1 14-ounce jar pizza sauce

1 8-ounce can tomato sauce

½ cup milk

¼ pound thinly sliced pepperoni

¼ cup diced Canadian bacon

1 teaspoon Italian seasoning

¾ teaspoon garlic powder

1 cup (4 ounces) shredded mozzarella

⅓ cup (about 2 ounces) freshly grated Parmigiano-Reggiano

¼ cup finely chopped fresh parsley

Preheat the oven to 350°F. Spray a 2½-quart baking dish with the vegetable oil spray.

Bring a large pot of water to a boil. Add the salt and penne and cook until tender but still firm to the bite, 8 to 10 minutes. Drain the pasta and set aside.

Heat a large skillet over medium heat. Add the sausage and onion and cook until the sausage is evenly browned and the onion is tender, 7 to 8 minutes. Carefully drain as much of the drippings as possible from the skillet. Set aside.

Combine the pizza sauce, tomato sauce, and milk in a large bowl. Stir in the sausage mixture, the pepperoni, Canadian bacon, Italian seasoning, and garlic powder. Add the pasta and stir gently until thoroughly coated with the sauce.

Transfer the pasta mixture to the prepared baking dish and sprinkle with the mozzarella and Parmigiano-Reggiano. Cover with aluminum foil and bake for 30 minutes. Remove the foil and continue to bake until the cheeses are melted and bubbly, about 15 minutes more. Garnish with the parsley and serve hot.

make it your own

Top the pasta with

- mushrooms
- olives
- roasted red peppers
- sun-dried tomatoes
- onions
- meatballs
- crumbled bacon
- artichokes

vegetable lasagne

Mom always made sure there were three things on our dinner plates: some meat (beef, pork, or chicken), a "starch" (potatoes or rice), and a vegetable (I always pushed back on those, but these days I find myself craving more vegetables). I often oven roast a pile of vegetables to a tender crispness or make this all-vegetable lasagne to satisfy my veggie cravings. With a blend of cheeses, a variety of vegetables, and plenty of seasonings, you won't miss the traditional meat sauce one bit.

MAKES 8 SERVINGS

2 tablespoons extra virgin olive oil

1 large yellow onion, diced

1 green bell pepper, cored, seeded, and diced

2 small zucchini, diced

2 small yellow summer squash, diced

1 head broccoli, florets separated and chopped

1 12-ounce jar roasted red peppers, drained and diced

½ teaspoon red pepper flakes

1 8-ounce log fresh goat cheese

8 ounces ricotta cheese

2 teaspoons minced garlic

1½ teaspoons chopped fresh thyme

1½ teaspoons dried basil

1½ teaspoons dried oregano

Kosher salt and freshly ground black pepper

4 cups Marinara Sauce (page 198)

1 pound no-boil lasagna noodles

½ cup (2 ounces) freshly grated Parmigiano-Reggiano

3 tablespoons chopped fresh parsley

Preheat the oven to 375°F. Grease a 9 x 13-inch ovenproof casserole dish.

Heat the olive oil in a large skillet over medium-high heat. Add the onion, bell pepper, zucchini, summer squash, and broccoli florets and cook for 3 to 5 minutes. Remove the vegetables from the heat and allow them to cool. Stir in the roasted red peppers and the red pepper flakes.

Mix the goat and ricotta cheeses in a medium bowl until well combined. Add the garlic, thyme, basil, and oregano and season with salt and pepper.

Spread 1 cup of the marinara sauce in the bottom of the prepared casserole dish. Arrange a layer of lasagna noodles over the sauce and season with pepper. Top with a layer of vegetables. Drop spoonfuls of the cheese mixture over the vegetables and spread the cheeses gently with a spatula, covering as much of the vegetables as you can. Repeat with the remaining sauce, noodles, vegetables, and cheese, finishing with a layer of lasagna noodles and sauce. Sprinkle the Parmigiano-Reggiano over the top.

Cover the lasagne with aluminum foil and bake for 45 minutes. Uncover and continue to bake until the top is browned, about 15 minutes. Let sit for 10 minutes before serving. Sprinkle with the parsley and serve.

three-cheese scalloped potatoes
with italian sausage

I can't think of a better made-in-heaven marriage than the one between a creamy cheese sauce and layers of thinly sliced potatoes. Traditionally served as a side dish with roast chicken or beef, scalloped potatoes can become a one-dish dinner when sausage is added to the mix.

MAKES 8 SERVINGS

Vegetable oil spray

¾ cup (3 ounces) shredded extra sharp white Cheddar

¾ cup (3 ounces) shredded Gruyère

⅓ cup (about 2 ounces) freshly grated Parmigiano-Reggiano

½ pound sweet Italian sausage, casings removed and sausage crumbled

4 tablespoons (½ stick) unsalted butter

¼ cup all-purpose flour

½ teaspoon dried thyme

2 teaspoons kosher salt

½ teaspoon freshly ground black pepper

3 cups milk

6 large baking potatoes, peeled and thinly sliced

¼ cup diced onion

Preheat the oven to 400°F. Spray a 7 x 11-inch baking dish with the vegetable oil spray.

Combine the Cheddar, Gruyère, and Parmigiano-Reggiano in a small bowl.

Heat a skillet over medium heat and add the sausage. Cook for 6 to 7 minutes, until the sausage is no longer pink. Drain off the drippings and set the sausage aside.

Melt the butter in a medium saucepan. Whisk in the flour, thyme, 1 teaspoon of the salt, and ¼ teaspoon of the pepper. Gradually whisk in the milk. Bring the mixture to a boil and cook, stirring, for 2 minutes. Reduce the heat to a low simmer. The sauce should be thick.

Arrange half of the potato slices, overlapping them slightly, in the prepared dish. Sprinkle with the remaining 1 teaspoon salt and ¼ teaspoon pepper. Scatter the onion and the sausage evenly over the potatoes, then top with half of the cheese mixture. Arrange the remaining potato slices over the top and sprinkle with the remaining cheese.

Pour the warm sauce evenly over the casserole and bake, uncovered, until the potatoes are tender, about 20 minutes. Let sit for 10 minutes before serving.

dishin' with DAVID

THIN IS IN

Professional chefs know how to make paper-thin, uniform slices of potatoes and other fruits and vegetables using a knife or an expensive—too expensive for most home cooks—piece of equipment called a mandoline. The good news is that there are now many inexpensive mandolines with finger guards on the market that are perfect for slicing potatoes, sausages, cucumbers, apples, carrots, and more. I use a mandoline whenever I make this dish or any others that call for piles of thinly sliced ingredients.

chicken potpie

Mom was a busy obstetrics nurse and sometimes found herself having to work late. To make sure we could feed ourselves on those days when she was running behind, Mom stocked the freezer with individual frozen potpies. I could barely wait for the timer to buzz to let me know that mine was ready. I remember poking a hole in the top of the hot crust with my spoon, smelling the rich aromas, and eating every bite of the tender chicken and vegetables blanketed in a velvety cream sauce. If you don't have time to roast a chicken, pick up an already-cooked rotisserie one at your market.

MAKES 6 TO 8 SERVINGS

PIE DOUGH

2½ cups all-purpose flour

1 teaspoon kosher salt

Pinch of sugar

½ pound (2 sticks) unsalted butter, very cold and cubed

CHICKEN

1 large onion, coarsely chopped

2 cups chopped carrots

1 leek, well rinsed and coarsely chopped

1 tablespoon extra virgin olive oil

1 3-pound whole chicken

4 celery stalks, coarsely chopped

6 fresh thyme sprigs

1 cup dry white wine

1 tablespoon kosher salt

1 teaspoon whole black peppercorns

1 tablespoon tomato paste

FILLING

1 tablespoon extra virgin olive oil

1 cup ½-inch sliced carrots

2 small onions, chopped

1 cup quartered button mushrooms

¼ cup sliced shiitake mushrooms (stems discarded)

1 cup fresh or frozen peas, thawed if frozen

2 teaspoons kosher salt

1 teaspoon freshly ground black pepper

8 tablespoons (1 stick) unsalted butter

¾ cup all-purpose flour

Leaves from 4 fresh thyme sprigs, chopped

Leaves from 2 fresh rosemary sprigs, chopped

1 large egg, lightly beaten

To make the pie dough, put the flour, salt, and sugar in the bowl of a food processor. Pulse 3 or 4 times to mix. Add the butter and pulse 6 to 8 times until the mixture resembles coarse meal. Add ¼ cup ice water, pulsing just until the dough holds together. Remove the dough, divide it into 2 equal-size balls, and wrap in plastic wrap. Refrigerate for 30 minutes to 1 hour.

Preheat the oven to 400°F.

To make the chicken, toss the onion, carrots, and leek with the olive oil on an aluminum foil–lined baking sheet. Roast for about 30 minutes, until golden and tender.

Transfer the vegetables to a Dutch oven. Add the chicken, celery, thyme, white wine, salt, and peppercorns. Add 8 cups water, enough to cover the chicken completely. Bring to a boil, then reduce the heat to low and simmer for 1 hour, until the chicken is tender when pierced with a fork.

Remove the chicken from the pot. When it is cool enough to handle, remove the meat from the bones and shred it, discarding the skin and bones. Strain the broth through a colander into a large pot and discard the solids. Stir the tomato paste into the broth and simmer over medium heat until the mixture has reduced to 6 cups, about 40 minutes.

To make the filling, heat the olive oil in a medium skillet. Add the carrots and onions and sauté until they begin to soften, 6 to 8 minutes. Add the button and shiitake mushrooms and sauté for 2 minutes. Add the peas, salt, and pepper and cook for 1 minute. Transfer the vegetables to a bowl.

In the same skillet, melt the butter over medium heat. Whisk in the flour and cook, whisking constantly, until the mixture is golden brown, about 10 minutes. Whisk in the thyme, rosemary, and the reserved broth. Add the shredded chicken and the vegetable mixture and bring to a simmer until the filling thickens, 5 to 8 minutes.

Remove the dough from the refrigerator. On a lightly floured surface, roll out 1 ball of dough into an 11 x 15 rectangle. Place the dough in the bottom of a 9- to 10-inch baking dish. (The dough should come up the sides of the dish.) Spread the chicken mixture over the dough. Roll out the remaining ball of dough into a 13-inch round. Place the dough on top of the chicken mixture. Using a fork or your fingers, pinch the edges to seal. Cut a 1-inch slit in the center of the crust to allow steam to escape. Brush the top crust with the beaten egg.

Place the potpie on a baking sheet and bake until the crust is golden brown and the filling is bubbling, about 45 minutes. Let cool on a wire rack for 5 minutes before serving.

day-after roast turkey
and stuffing casserole

I've long been a believer that most food tastes even better the day *after* it's made. I always make plenty, much more than I need to serve my family and friends, so there are lots of leftovers to turn into more great meals. This turkey, stuffing, and cranberry sauce casserole makes those warm feelings that started on Thanksgiving Thursday last all weekend long.

MAKES 4 SERVINGS

1 tablespoon unsalted butter, at room
   temperature
4 cups cooked stuffing
¼ pound green beans, cut into 1-inch
   pieces and blanched

2 to 3 cups cooked and chopped turkey
1½ cups turkey gravy
½ cup slivered almonds
2 tablespoons chopped fresh parsley
½ to ¾ cup cranberry sauce

Preheat the oven to 350°F. Grease a 3-quart baking dish with the butter.

   Spread 2 cups of the stuffing in the bottom of the dish, followed by the green beans, turkey, and the remaining 2 cups stuffing. Pour the gravy on top. Sprinkle on the almonds and parsley. Spoon dollops of cranberry sauce on top. Bake for 30 minutes, or until hot throughout. Let the casserole sit for 5 minutes before serving.

turkey shepherd's pie

When I stop at a roadside diner, I frequently order shepherd's pie, a dish of ground beef or lamb and vegetables with a mashed potato topping. I can't wait to push my fork through the browned potato "crust" to get to all the good things underneath.

When I make shepherd's pie at home, I lighten it up by using ground turkey instead of beef or lamb. I prefer a blend of light and dark meat turkey so the dish stays tender and moist.

MAKES 8 SERVINGS

6 to 8 large baking potatoes, peeled and quartered

⅓ cup (about 3 ounces) sour cream

⅓ cup milk

3 tablespoons unsalted butter

2 teaspoons freshly ground black pepper

1 teaspoon kosher salt

1 tablespoon extra virgin olive oil

2 small onions, chopped

3 pounds ground turkey

1 green bell pepper, cored, seeded, and chopped

3 carrots, chopped

1 tablespoon chopped fresh parsley

¼ teaspoon dried thyme

1 garlic clove, minced

¾ cup low-sodium chicken broth

3 tablespoons all-purpose flour

1 teaspoon paprika

Place the potatoes in a large pot and add enough water to cover. Bring the water to a boil and cook until the potatoes are tender when pierced with a fork, about 20 minutes.

Drain the potatoes and return them to the pot. Using a potato masher, mash the potatoes until no lumps remain. Add the sour cream, milk, butter, pepper, and salt. Continue mashing until all the ingredients are well combined. Set aside.

Preheat the broiler.

Heat the olive oil in a large skillet over medium heat. Add the onions and sauté until softened. Stir in the turkey, bell pepper, carrots, parsley, thyme, and garlic and cook over medium heat for about 5 minutes, until cooked through. Add the remaining salt and pepper. Pour the chicken broth into a small bowl and whisk in the flour. Pour the stock mixture into the skillet and cook until heated through and thickened, 8 to 10 minutes. Transfer the turkey mixture to a broiler-proof 4-quart rectangular baking dish.

Spread the mashed potatoes evenly over the turkey mixture, making sure to get all the way to the edges. Broil the casserole until the topping is golden brown, 5 to 7 minutes. Sprinkle with the paprika before serving.

chicken enchilada casserole

If you're looking to get dinner on the table in fewer than thirty minutes, try this traditional Tex-Mex favorite. With some leftover chicken, easy-to-find ingredients, and short prep time, this takes care of a hungry family on a busy weeknight.

MAKES 6 SERVINGS

Vegetable oil spray
6 7-inch flour tortillas
2 10-ounce cans enchilada sauce, such as
    Old El Paso
1 cup (8 ounces) sour cream
1 4.5-ounce can chopped green chiles,
    drained

3 cups cooked and shredded chicken
3 cups (12 ounces) shredded Monterey
    Jack
2 tablespoons chopped fresh cilantro

Preheat the oven to 350°F.

Spray a skillet with the vegetable oil spray and heat over medium-high heat. One at a time, add the tortillas to the skillet and cook, turning them every 30 to 40 seconds, until they are well toasted. Using tongs, transfer them to a cutting board to cool. When cool enough to handle, slice them into strips 1 to 2 inches wide.

Whisk together 1 cup of the enchilada sauce, the sour cream, and green chiles in a medium bowl. Stir in the shredded chicken.

Spread a thin layer of the remaining enchilada sauce in the bottom of a 9 x 13-inch baking dish. Add a layer of tortilla strips, followed by half of the chicken mixture and one third of the Jack cheese. Repeat layering with the tortilla strips, enchilada sauce, and Jack cheese. Cover the casserole with aluminum foil and bake for 15 minutes. Remove the foil and bake until the cheese is bubbling, 5 to 10 minutes more. Remove from the oven and let sit for 5 minutes. Sprinkle with cilantro before serving.

chicken
═══ birds of a feather ═══

I FIND THAT CHICKEN is too often underrated. That's because it's usually prepared in the same old ways. For me, chicken is the most versatile meat I can think of. It can be braised, deep-fried, sautéed, grilled, roasted, used in potpies, or baked under a blanket of sauce. You can cook a whole bird or just your favorite parts. Chicken can be used in appetizers, tossed into salads for light lunches, piled on your favorite bread for overstuffed sandwiches, and served at a family supper or at the most elegant dinner parties.

If you're like me, hungry for new chicken ideas, here are some creative recipes that work for quick lunches, casual dinners, and formal meals.

down-home
southern fried chicken

I can't think of any dish that's more satisfying and comforting than fried chicken. Straight out of the skillet, it's crispy, crunchy on the outside, moist and juicy on the inside.

MAKES 4 TO 6 SERVINGS

BUTTERMILK BRINE

4 cups buttermilk

2 tablespoons hot sauce

1 tablespoon kosher salt

1 tablespoon freshly ground black pepper

CHICKEN

1 3- to 4-pound chicken, cut up into 8 pieces

2 cups all-purpose flour

1 teaspoon dried thyme

1 teaspoon dried marjoram

2 teaspoons onion powder

1 teaspoon garlic powder

½ teaspoon cayenne

1 tablespoon kosher salt

1 tablespoon freshly ground black pepper

Canola oil for frying

To make the brine, whisk together the buttermilk, hot sauce, salt, and pepper in a dish shallow enough to hold the chicken in a single layer. Add the chicken pieces, cover, and refrigerate for at least 3 hours. Turn the chicken once while marinating.

Pour the chicken into a colander and allow the brine to drain.

Place the flour, thyme, marjoram, onion powder, garlic powder, cayenne, salt, and black pepper in a resealable plastic bag. Put 2 or 3 of the chicken pieces in the bag, close, and shake well to coat. Remove the chicken from the flour mixture and shake off any excess. Repeat with the remaining chicken. Place the chicken on a wire rack, while heating the oil.

Heat 2 to 2½ inches of canola oil to 350°F in a cast-iron or other deep skillet. The skillet should be large enough to hold the chicken in a single layer without touching. Add the chicken to the hot oil. Cook for 7 to 9 minutes. Using tongs, turn the chicken and cook the other side for an additional 7 to 9 minutes. Remove the chicken to a wire rack set over paper towels. To test for doneness, an instant-read thermometer inserted into the thickest piece of chicken should register 165°F. If not, return the chicken to the hot oil for another 2 to 3 minutes and test again. Let the chicken rest for 5 to 10 minutes before serving.

dishin' with DAVID

PERFECT FRIED CHICKEN

• Don't skip the buttermilk brine; it tenderizes the chicken and helps the flour stick to the skin.

• Shake off any excess flour after dredging, so the crust isn't too thick.

• Keep the hot oil at a constant temperature of 350°F throughout cooking. Maintain an even temperature by clipping a deep-frying thermometer to the pan.

down-home
southern fried chicken

I can't think of any dish that's more satisfying and comforting than fried chicken. Straight out of the skillet, it's crispy, crunchy on the outside, moist and juicy on the inside.

MAKES 4 TO 6 SERVINGS

BUTTERMILK BRINE

4 cups buttermilk

2 tablespoons hot sauce

1 tablespoon kosher salt

1 tablespoon freshly ground black pepper

CHICKEN

1 3- to 4-pound chicken, cut up into 8 pieces

2 cups all-purpose flour

1 teaspoon dried thyme

1 teaspoon dried marjoram

2 teaspoons onion powder

1 teaspoon garlic powder

½ teaspoon cayenne

1 tablespoon kosher salt

1 tablespoon freshly ground black pepper

Canola oil for frying

To make the brine, whisk together the buttermilk, hot sauce, salt, and pepper in a dish shallow enough to hold the chicken in a single layer. Add the chicken pieces, cover, and refrigerate for at least 3 hours. Turn the chicken once while marinating.

Pour the chicken into a colander and allow the brine to drain.

Place the flour, thyme, marjoram, onion powder, garlic powder, cayenne, salt, and black pepper in a resealable plastic bag. Put 2 or 3 of the chicken pieces in the bag, close, and shake well to coat. Remove the chicken from the flour mixture and shake off any excess. Repeat with the remaining chicken. Place the chicken on a wire rack, while heating the oil.

Heat 2 to 2½ inches of canola oil to 350°F in a cast-iron or other deep skillet. The skillet should be large enough to hold the chicken in a single layer without touching. Add the chicken to the hot oil. Cook for 7 to 9 minutes. Using tongs, turn the chicken and cook the other side for an additional 7 to 9 minutes. Remove the chicken to a wire rack set over paper towels. To test for doneness, an instant-read thermometer inserted into the thickest piece of chicken should register 165°F. If not, return the chicken to the hot oil for another 2 to 3 minutes and test again. Let the chicken rest for 5 to 10 minutes before serving.

dishin' with DAVID

PERFECT FRIED CHICKEN

- Don't skip the buttermilk brine; it tenderizes the chicken and helps the flour stick to the skin.
- Shake off any excess flour after dredging, so the crust isn't too thick.
- Keep the hot oil at a constant temperature of 350°F throughout cooking. Maintain an even temperature by clipping a deep-frying thermometer to the pan.

Make it your own

- For thicker gravy, whisk together ¼ cup broth with ¼ cup flour until smooth and then stir it back into the pot.
- Add ½ cup chopped fresh herbs, such as parsley, dill, chives, or rosemary, to the batter.
- Add chopped scallions to the batter.

mimi's chicken and dumplings

Both of my grandmothers made chicken and dumplings, as does Mom, but I have to confess that Grandmother Mimi's was my favorite. I have vivid memories of watching her make this winter mainstay whenever we went across town to visit her. It was quite a production. First, she simmered a chicken to make fresh broth and then shredded the meat. To make the dumplings, she piled some flour on her wooden cutting board and made a well in the center. Then she ladled some broth into the well, using her hand to mix the dough. With her big rolling pin, she rolled out the dough and cut out the dumplings. Then she gently dropped them into the chicken and broth.

Mimi's homemade dumplings were the best, but when time is short, I found a surefire stand-in. I call them whomp 'em biscuits because you peel the paper off a tube of refrigerated biscuits and then whomp 'em against the counter to open the package. The biscuits are floured, rolled flat, and cut into squares, then added to the broth. This is a comfort-food favorite.

MAKES 6 SERVINGS

BROTH

3 tablespoons extra virgin olive oil

1 large onion, diced small

3 carrots, diced small

4 celery stalks, diced small

1 2½- to 3- pound whole or cut-up chicken

1 teaspoon chopped fresh parsley

½ teaspoon dried thyme

2 bay leaves

4 cups low-sodium chicken broth

Salt

Black pepper to taste

DUMPLINGS

1 16.3-ounce tube (8 biscuits) Pillsbury
    Grands! Flaky Layers

¾ cup all-purpose flour

To make the broth, heat the olive oil in a stockpot over medium heat. Add the onion, carrots, and celery and sauté until tender, 6 to 8 minutes. Add the chicken, parsley, thyme, bay leaves, and chicken broth. Add enough water to cover all the ingredients. Bring to a boil and then immediately reduce to a simmer. Simmer until the chicken is tender, 1½ hours. Using tongs, remove the chicken from the broth to a bowl and allow to cool. Remove and discard the bay leaves.

When the chicken is cool enough to handle, remove the meat and cut or tear it into strips. Discard the skin and bones. Add the chicken meat and broth to the stockpot and bring back to a simmer while making the dumplings. Season with a pinch of salt and some pepper.

To make the dumplings, generously flour both sides of the biscuits. On a floured work surface, roll out each of the biscuits to a thickness of ⅛ to ¼ inch. Cut each biscuit into 1½-inch strips. Gently lower the strips into the simmering broth. The biscuits will pop up to the surface and then fall back down into the broth. Stir gently, allowing the dumplings to separate. Allow the dumplings to simmer for 10 to 12 minutes, until soft. Ladle the chicken, dumplings, and broth into soup bowls and serve.

chicken
=== birds of a feather ===

I FIND THAT CHICKEN is too often underrated. That's because it's usually prepared in the same old ways. For me, chicken is the most versatile meat I can think of. It can be braised, deep-fried, sautéed, grilled, roasted, used in potpies, or baked under a blanket of sauce. You can cook a whole bird or just your favorite parts. Chicken can be used in appetizers, tossed into salads for light lunches, piled on your favorite bread for overstuffed sandwiches, and served at a family supper or at the most elegant dinner parties.

If you're like me, hungry for new chicken ideas, here are some creative recipes that work for quick lunches, casual dinners, and formal meals.

southern barbecued chicken

I love having friends over and serving them this tangy chicken outside on the picnic table. The vinegary, smoky sauce is a little messy by design, but when eating any kind of barbecue, I always say if you don't get the sauce all over your face, you're doing it wrong! Making barbecued chicken is tricky; if just grilled it can often become burned on the outside, pink on the inside. My solution is to start the chicken in the oven so it cooks through and then finish it on the grill for a nice char. Some Skillet Corn Bread with Scallions and Cheddar (page 32) and Creamy Potato Salad with Bacon (page 90) round out the meal.

MAKES 6 TO 8 SERVINGS

MARINADE

½ cup canola oil

Juice of 1 lemon

3 tablespoons red wine vinegar

2 tablespoons low-sodium soy sauce

2 teaspoons garlic powder

1 teaspoon dried thyme

1 3½-pound chicken, cut into 8 pieces

BARBECUE SAUCE

1 cup ketchup

¼ cup packed dark brown sugar

2 tablespoons apple cider vinegar

1 teaspoon Worcestershire sauce

¼ teaspoon liquid smoke

½ teaspoon dry mustard

½ teaspoon paprika

½ teaspoon chili powder

¼ teaspoon cayenne pepper

To make the marinade, whisk together the canola oil, lemon juice, vinegar, soy sauce, garlic powder, and thyme. Arrange the chicken in a single layer in a shallow baking dish. Pour the marinade over the chicken to coat on all sides. Cover with plastic wrap and refrigerate for 2 to 4 hours.

Preheat the oven to 350°F.

Remove the chicken pieces from the marinade and arrange in a single layer in a baking dish. Bake the chicken for 25 to 30 minutes and remove it from the oven. The chicken will not be cooked through.

To make the barbecue sauce, whisk together the ketchup, brown sugar, vinegar, Worcestershire sauce, liquid smoke, mustard, paprika, chili powder, and cayenne in a bowl. Put half of the sauce in a separate saucepan to reheat later and serve with the chicken.

Brush the grill grate lightly with oil and preheat the grill. When the grill is hot, place the chicken on the grate and grill for 3 to 5 minutes on each side. Baste the chicken with the barbecue sauce and grill on each side for 5 to 7 minutes more. To test for doneness, insert an instant-read thermometer into the thickest part of a piece of the chicken, but don't let the thermometer touch the bone. The chicken is fully cooked when the thermometer reads 165°F.

To cook the chicken indoors, remove the chicken from the oven after 25 to 30 minutes. Brush the sauce on the chicken and bake for 20 to 25 minutes more, until an instant-read thermometer says 165°F.

Reheat the reserved sauce and serve with the chicken.

herb-roasted chicken

Every home cook needs a great roast chicken recipe. My secret to perfect roast chicken is to rub some butter mixed with other ingredients under the skin *and* add some seasonings to the cavity as well. The results: crisp, salty skin; moist breast meat; and dense dark meat. Once you try this method, you'll never roast a chicken any other way. I like my roast chicken with some Creamy Garlic Mashed Potatoes (page 107) and a side of steamed broccoli.

MAKES 4 TO 6 SERVINGS

1 5-pound chicken

¼ cup extra virgin olive oil

1½ cups mixed and minced fresh herbs, such as basil, parsley, thyme, marjoram, and oregano

2 garlic cloves, minced

1 tablespoon kosher salt

1 tablespoon freshly ground black pepper

1 lemon, halved

1 fresh rosemary sprig

1 bay leaf

¼ teaspoon lemon pepper seasoning (optional)

Preheat the oven to 400°F.

Rinse the chicken and pat it dry with paper towels.

Combine the olive oil, herbs, and garlic in a small bowl. Slip a finger between the meat and the skin at the chicken's large cavity. Gently work your fingers up one breast to loosen the skin, then do the same to the other one. With your fingers, evenly spread as much of the herb mixture under the skin as you can. Season the chicken inside and out with the salt and pepper. Stuff the cavity with the lemon halves, rosemary sprig, bay leaf, lemon pepper seasoning (if using), and any leftover herbs. Gently pull the skin down over the breast so that none of the meat is exposed. Tuck in the wings under the breasts and tie the legs together with kitchen twine. Put the chicken on a rack in a roasting pan.

Loosely cover the chicken's breasts with aluminum foil. Roast the chicken for 1½ hours. Remove the foil and continue to roast the chicken for 15 to 20 minutes more, until an instant-read thermometer inserted into the thickest part of the chicken reads 165°F. Transfer the chicken to a cutting board, and let it stand at room temperature for 10 to 15 minutes before carving and serving.

make it your own

- Use favorite herbs and seasoning and mix with the butter.
- Slip thinly sliced mushrooms or goat cheese with herbs under the skin.

chicken alfredo
with broccoli

As a kid, I didn't care too much for broccoli. I vividly remember when I was in high school and we went to dinner at an Italian restaurant where this pasta dish was on the menu. When I read the description of the tender chicken and broccoli in a creamy cheese sauce, I figured I could just push the broccoli aside if I didn't like it. To my surprise, the broccoli was perfectly cooked—tender, yet crisp—and I loved it. I realized what I had been missing and have been eating my broccoli ever since. A basket of soft, warm garlic bread sticks makes a nice addition.

MAKES 6 SERVINGS

2 teaspoons plus 1 teaspoon kosher salt

1 head broccoli, separated into florets

12 ounces penne or bowtie pasta

2 tablespoons extra virgin olive oil

4 skinless, boneless chicken breast halves, cut into ½-inch strips

½ teaspoon freshly ground black pepper

2 tablespoons dry white wine

2 garlic cloves, minced

1⅔ cups heavy cream

1½ cups plus 2 tablespoons freshly grated Parmigiano-Reggiano

1 cup (4 ounces) grated Italian Fontina

Bring a large pot of water and 2 teaspoons of the salt to a boil. Add the broccoli florets and cook for 1 to 2 minutes. Using a hand strainer, remove the broccoli from the boiling water and run it under cold water to stop the cooking.

Using the same boiling water, cook the penne until tender but still firm to the bite, 6 to 8 minutes. Drain and set aside.

Heat the olive oil in a Dutch oven over medium-high heat. Season the chicken with the remaining 1 teaspoon salt and the pepper. Working in batches, sauté the chicken strips until just cooked through, about 4 minutes. Transfer the chicken to a bowl.

Add the white wine and garlic to the Dutch oven and bring to a simmer over medium heat. Cook for 1 minute, scraping up any browned bits from the bottom of the pot. Stir in the cream. Slowly add 1½ cups of the Parmigiano-Reggiano and all the Fontina, stirring constantly. Cook over low heat until the cheese has melted and the sauce has thickened slightly, 5 to 10 minutes. (The cheese shouldn't stick to the bottom of the pot.) Add the chicken mixture and any accumulated juices, the broccoli, and penne and toss until the mixture is well coated and heated through, about 3 minutes. Taste for seasoning. Divide among pasta bowls and sprinkle with the remaining 2 tablespoons Parmesan before serving.

chicken parmesan

This classic incorporates everything I love about Italian-American food—panfried chicken cutlets baked under a blanket of zesty tomato sauce and tangy cheeses. It reminds me of cozy restaurants with red-and-white-checked tablecloths and a candle melting down the sides of a straw-covered Chianti bottle. Create your own evening of Italian comfort with this dish. Serve it the old-fashioned way with a side of spaghetti tossed with tomato sauce.

MAKES 4 SERVINGS

SAUCE

¼ cup extra virgin olive oil

½ large yellow onion, chopped

2 medium garlic cloves, minced

1 28-ounce can crushed tomatoes

1 teaspoon dried oregano

Pinch of red pepper flakes

½ teaspoon kosher salt

CHICKEN

4 boneless, skinless chicken breast cutlets
(¼ inch thick)

Kosher salt

1 cup all-purpose flour

3 large eggs

1 cup fresh bread crumbs

1 cup (4 ounces) freshly grated
Parmigiano-Reggiano

¼ cup extra virgin olive oil

8 ounces mozzarella, thinly sliced

2 tablespoons minced fresh basil

To make the sauce, heat the olive oil in a saucepan over medium heat. Add the onion and sauté until softened, about 3 minutes. Add the garlic and cook until fragrant, about 1 minute more. Add the tomatoes, oregano, red pepper flakes and salt, and bring to a simmer. Simmer the sauce while preparing the chicken, about 10 minutes. Let the sauce cool for 15 minutes. Pour the sauce into a food processor or blender and purée until smooth.

Preheat the oven to 350°F.

Season the chicken with salt.

Put the flour on a shallow plate. On another shallow plate, whisk the eggs until well combined. On a third plate, combine the bread crumbs, ½ cup of the Parmigiano-Reggiano, and a pinch of salt.

Heat the olive oil over medium-high heat in a skillet large enough to hold the chicken in a single layer. Dredge a cutlet in the flour, then dip in the beaten egg, and then dredge in the bread crumb mixture. Transfer the chicken to the skillet. Repeat with the remaining cutlets. Reduce the heat to medium and fry the chicken until it is golden brown, about 3 minutes on each side.

Spread a thick layer of tomato sauce in the bottom of a 9 x 13-baking dish. Arrange the chicken in a single layer on top of the sauce. Pour another layer of sauce evenly over the chicken. Top with the mozzarella and the remaining ½ cup Parmigiano-Reggiano. Bake until the mozzarella is just beginning to brown, 10 to 12 minutes. Let the chicken sit for 5 minutes. Sprinkle on the basil before serving.

THIN IS IN

Ever notice how some chicken cutlets can be meaty in the middle, thinner at the ends. They'll cook more evenly if they all are the same thickness. You can ask your butcher to flatten the chicken breasts, but it's so easy to do it yourself. Place the chicken cutlets in a single layer between two sheets of plastic wrap or in a plastic bag. Using the bottom of your heaviest skillet—cast iron preferred—give the chicken a few good whacks.

lemon chicken

Bright and light, this refreshing chicken pops with lemony flavor. I often serve this for a weekend lunch, accompanied by some grilled or steamed asparagus or sugar snap peas. I often round out the plate by adding some fluffy rice.

MAKES 8 SERVINGS

1 3½- to 4-pound chicken, cut up into 8 pieces

1 teaspoon plus 1½ teaspoons kosher salt

1 teaspoon plus 1 teaspoon freshly ground black pepper

2 tablespoons finely grated lemon zest

½ cup fresh lemon juice

2 garlic cloves, crushed

2 teaspoons dried thyme

4 tablespoons (½ stick) unsalted butter, melted

2 lemons, thinly sliced

½ cup chopped fresh parsley

4 to 5 cups cooked white rice

Arrange the chicken in a single layer in a shallow baking dish. Season with 1 teaspoon of the salt and 1 teaspoon of the pepper.

Whisk together the lemon zest, lemon juice, garlic, thyme, the remaining 1½ teaspoons salt, and the remaining 1 teaspoon pepper in a bowl and pour over the chicken. Cover with plastic wrap and refrigerate for 3 to 4 hours, turning occasionally.

Preheat the oven to 425°F.

Drain the marinade and reserve 1 cup, leaving the chicken in the baking dish. Brush the chicken with the melted butter. Bake for 25 minutes, then brush with some of the reserved marinade. Continue to bake until the chicken is browned and cooked through, about 30 minutes more.

Remove the chicken from the oven. Garnish with the lemon slices and sprinkle with the parsley. Serve the chicken with the cooked rice.

chicken marsala

Thin chicken cutlets topped with a velvety sauce of mushrooms, cream, and marsala wine from Sicily are a perfect example of how comfort food can be elegant as well as homey. When I am hosting an elegant dinner party, this easy preparation is one of my go-to favorites. A steamed green vegetable—broccoli, snow peas, asparagus, or green beans—adds color.

MAKES 4 SERVINGS

3 tablespoons unsalted butter

2 tablespoons finely chopped shallots

10 ounces cremini mushrooms, halved

1 cup all-purpose flour

1 teaspoon kosher salt

½ teaspoon freshly ground black pepper

2 teaspoons chopped fresh thyme

2 tablespoons extra virgin olive oil

4 boneless, skinless chicken cutlets, pounded to ¼-inch thickness

1 cup low-sodium chicken broth

½ cup marsala wine

⅔ cup heavy cream

1½ teaspoons fresh lemon juice

¼ cup chopped fresh parsley

Preheat the oven to 250°F.

Melt the butter in a skillet over medium heat. Add the shallots and sauté until they begin to turn golden, about 1 minute. Add the mushrooms and cook until they are soft and brown, 6 to 8 minutes. Remove the mushrooms and shallots from the skillet to a small bowl and set aside.

Combine the flour, salt, pepper, and thyme in a shallow dish.

Using the same skillet, heat the olive oil over medium-high heat. Dredge the chicken cutlets, shake off any excess flour, and add to the skillet. Sauté the chicken for 2 to 3 minutes. Turn once and sauté for 2 to 3 minutes more. Remove the chicken to a dish and keep warm in the oven.

Add the chicken broth and marsala wine to the same skillet and bring to a boil, stirring up the browned bits on the bottom of the pan. Lower the heat and simmer for about 2 minutes. Stir in the cream, lemon juice, and the mushroom mixture. Divide the chicken among four plates and top with the sauce and parsley before serving.

dishin' with DAVID

UNCORK THE SECRETS

When it comes to choosing what wine to drink with food, chef, vintner, and author Michael Chiarello shared the following with me: "The only rule is to drink what you like and like what you drink. If you think about it, there are a lot of people who like to pair strong flavors with strong flavors. I like to contrast. If I have something rich, I want something bright and acidic with it that can cut through. I want the wine to get me prepared for the next bite; not my bite to get me prepared for the next sip. Sauvignon blanc is like the golden retriever of white wine. It likes whatever you're cooking and it's got enough body and acid to go across the board."

chicken cacciatore

Chicken cacciatore is a rustic Italian chicken stew with tomatoes and vegetables. Hearty cremini mushrooms are used here, but feel free to choose a mix of button, portobello, or shiitake. Serve it on pasta, mashed potatoes, or polenta.

MAKES 6 SERVINGS

1½ pounds (about 4 cups) plum tomatoes, coarsely chopped

8 ounces cremini mushrooms, halved or quartered if large

1 large yellow onion, diced

1 large green bell pepper, cored, seeded, and diced

1 large red bell pepper, cored, seeded, and diced

¼ cup extra virgin olive oil

2 tablespoons sherry vinegar

Kosher salt and freshly ground black pepper

1 4-pound chicken, cut up into 8 pieces

2 garlic cloves, minced

½ cup dry red wine

1 14.5-ounce can crushed tomatoes

1 cup low-sodium chicken broth

¼ cup tomato paste

1½ tablespoons chopped fresh rosemary

1 tablespoon chopped fresh thyme

2 tablespoons capers, drained

12 ounces gemelli or penne

½ cup chopped fresh basil

Preheat the oven to 450°F.

Combine the plum tomatoes, mushrooms, onion, green bell peppers, and red bell pepper in a large bowl. Add 2 tablespoons of the olive oil and the sherry vinegar and toss to combine. Season generously with salt and pepper. Spread the vegetables on a baking sheet in a single layer. Roast until the vegetables are tender when pierced with a fork, 30 to 45 minutes. Remove the vegetables from the oven and set aside. Reduce the oven temperature to 325°F.

Season the chicken with salt and pepper. Heat the remaining 2 tablespoons olive oil in a Dutch oven over medium-high heat. Add the chicken, skin side down, and cook until the skin is golden brown, 4 to 6 minutes. Flip over the chicken pieces and cook for 4 to 6 minutes more. Transfer the chicken to a bowl.

Add the garlic and red wine to the pot and bring to a boil. Boil until the mixture is reduced by half, scraping up any browned bits from the bottom of the pot, about 1 minute. Stir in the crushed tomatoes and their juices, the chicken broth, and tomato paste and bring to a boil. Reduce the heat to medium and simmer until the flavors are blended, about 10 minutes.

Add the chicken to the pot, skin side up. Cover the pot, transfer it to the oven, and roast for 25 to 30 minutes. Uncover and continue to roast for 15 to 20 minutes more. Remove the pot from the oven and stir in the roasted vegetables, the rosemary, thyme, and 1 tablespoon of the capers. Return the pot to the oven and roast until the vegetables are heated through, about 5 minutes.

While the chicken is cooking, bring a large pot of salted water to a boil and cook the gemelli until tender but still firm to the bite.

Divide the pasta among serving bowls. Top each bowl with some of the chicken, vegetables, and sauce. Sprinkle with the basil and the remaining 1 tablespoon capers before serving.

chicken cordon bleu

For Chicken Cordon Bleu, a flattened boneless chicken breast is filled with ham and cheese, then rolled in bread crumbs and fried. In my easy-to-prepare version, all of the ingredients are combined with a creamy sauce, placed in individual ovenproof bowls, and topped with a round of store-bought puff pastry for a beautiful presentation. Make the filling and cut out the pastry rounds a day ahead and you can pop these into the oven for a midweek dinner. Pair it with some sautéed broccoli rabe and steamed rice.

MAKES 8 SERVINGS

2 tablespoons unsalted butter

1 medium onion, diced

3 garlic cloves, minced

2 tablespoons chopped fresh rosemary

1 teaspoon paprika

½ cup (4 ounces) cubed cream cheese, at room temperature

¼ cup low-sodium chicken broth

1 3- to 4-pound rotisserie chicken, meat removed and shredded

2 cups (about 1 pound) finely diced smoked ham

2 cups (about ½ pound) finely diced Swiss cheese

1½ teaspoons chopped fresh parsley

1½ teaspoons kosher salt

1 teaspoon freshly ground black pepper

2 packages (4 sheets) store-bought frozen puff pastry, thawed

1 large egg

1 tablespoon milk

Preheat the oven to 400°F.

Melt the butter in a large skillet over medium heat. Add the onion, garlic, rosemary, and paprika and cook until the onion has softened, 4 to 5 minutes. Stir in the cream cheese and chicken broth and continue to cook until the cream cheese melts. Stir in the chicken and ham and cook until just warmed through.

Remove the pan from the heat and add the Swiss cheese, tossing to combine. Stir in the parsley. Season with the salt and pepper. Divide the mixture among four 8-ounce individual ramekins or soufflé dishes.

Unfold the thawed puff pastry on a lightly floured surface. Using a floured rolling pin, roll the pastry out to a thickness of ¼ inch. Cut out 8 circles slightly larger in diameter than the ramekins being used. Whisk the egg and milk together in a small bowl. Dab the rim of the ramekins with the egg wash before placing one circle of pastry over the crock. Lightly pinch the edges to adhere. Brush the puff pastry with the egg wash. Bake until the pastry is golden brown, 12 to 15 minutes. Let rest for 5 minutes before serving.

beef
=== mighty meaty ===

WHEN I THINK about hearty comfort food, beef is at the top of my list. I love the variety that beef offers, and whether you choose roasts, ribs, or steaks, there's something for everyone.

What's important to remember is that each cut of beef benefits from being cooked in a specific way. Lean tenderloin roasts shine when seared on the cooktop and then quickly roasted to rare juiciness. Tougher cuts, such as brisket, short ribs, and bottom round roasts, are best when cooked low and slow for hours until fork-tender. And, of course, there are endless comforting ways to prepare ground beef: meat loaves, sloppy Joes, and meatballs, to name a few. And don't you love it when you to go the fridge the next day and find just enough leftovers—two slices of meat loaf, a few meatballs, or some roast beef—to make yourself a big old sandwich?

sage and rosemary–rubbed beef tenderloin

Guests are so impressed when you serve a buttery, melt-in-your-mouth beef tenderloin. For hosts, it's a no-fail main course. It cooks quickly—in fewer than 30 minutes—and it's easy to carve. What many people don't realize is that filet mignons are individual thick slices of the tenderloin. For me, there's no better way to season beef than with sage and rosemary. I like to serve Creamy Garlic Mashed Potatoes (page 107) and steamed snow peas with this roast.

MAKES 8 TO 10 SERVINGS

MARINADE

½ cup extra virgin olive oil

¼ cup minced shallots

¼ cup minced garlic

3 fresh rosemary sprigs

1 fresh sage sprig

½ teaspoon freshly ground black pepper

SAUCE

4 tablespoons (½ stick) unsalted butter

1 tablespoon extra virgin olive oil

¼ cup finely chopped shallots

¼ cup minced garlic

1 cup dry red wine

2 teaspoons minced fresh rosemary

2 tablespoons minced fresh sage

1 teaspoon kosher salt, plus more to taste

1 teaspoon freshly ground black pepper,
   plus more to taste

1 cup beef stock

1 4- to 5-pound trimmed beef tenderloin

2 teaspoons kosher salt

2 teaspoons freshly ground black pepper

2 tablespoons extra virgin olive oil

2 fresh rosemary sprigs

2 to 3 fresh sage leaves

To make the marinade, combine the olive oil, shallots, garlic, rosemary, sage, and pepper in a large plastic bag. Add the beef, close the bag, and allow the meat to marinate in the refrigerator for at least 1 hour or overnight.

To make the sauce, melt 2 tablespoons of the butter with the olive oil in a large saucepan over medium-low heat. Add the shallots and garlic and sauté until softened, 3 minutes. Add the red wine, rosemary, sage, 1 teaspoon salt, and 1 teaspoon pepper and bring to a boil. Cook until the wine evaporates, about 1 minute. Add the beef stock and bring to a simmer. Cook until the mixture reduces to 1½ cups, about 20 minutes. Strain the mixture into a medium saucepan, pressing on the solids to extract as much liquid as possible. Discard the solids. (The sauce can be made 24 to 36 hours in advance. Cool slightly, then cover and refrigerate.)

To roast the beef, remove the meat from the marinade and let it stand at room temperature for 1 hour.

Preheat the oven to 350°F.

Season the beef with the salt and pepper. Heat the olive oil in a large heavy-bottomed oven-proof skillet over high heat. Add the beef and sear on all sides until well browned. Add the rosemary and sage. Roast until an instant-read thermometer inserted into the thickest part of the meat registers 125°F for medium-rare (it will be 135°F to 140°F in the thinnest part), about 30 minutes. Remove the beef from the oven and allow it to rest for 15 minutes.

Bring the sauce to a boil and whisk in the remaining 2 tablespoons butter. Season to taste with salt and pepper.

Slice the beef into ½-inch-thick slices. Arrange the slices on a warm platter and pass the sauce on the side.

Make it your own

Compound butters
- parsley, lemon juice, and zest
- shallots
- herbs
- chipotles in adobe
- blue cheese and bacon
- mustard
- prepared horseradish
- sun-dried tomato paste
- mushrooms
- Cajun spice mix
- smoked paprika
- nuts
- cilantro and cumin
- olives

marinated rib-eye steaks
with gorgonzola butter

A well-marbled rib-eye has always been my favorite steak. I briefly marinate them in herbs, garlic, and olive oil and then cook them in a really hot skillet. The final touch is a pat of Gorgonzola butter placed on each steak before serving. Of course, the steaks can be grilled on a preheated outdoor grill. Cook them for 6 to 10 minutes per side, depending on desired doneness.

MAKES 4 SERVINGS

STEAKS

3 tablespoons chopped fresh parsley

1 tablespoon minced garlic

2 teaspoons minced fresh thyme

½ cup extra virgin olive oil

1 teaspoon kosher salt

4 8- to 10-ounce bone-in rib-eye steaks

GORGONZOLA BUTTER

1 garlic clove

8 tablespoons (1 stick) unsalted butter, at room temperature

2 tablespoons crumbled Gorgonzola

2 tablespoons cream cheese, at room temperature

2 tablespoons chopped fresh basil

To marinate the steaks, whisk together the parsley, garlic, thyme, olive oil, and salt in a small bowl. Arrange the steaks in a single layer in a shallow dish. Pour the marinade over the steaks, cover the dish, and refrigerate for 1 to 2 hours—any longer and the steaks will become mushy.

While the steaks are marinating, prepare the Gorgonzola butter. Put the garlic in a food processor and pulse until it is coarsely chopped. Add the butter, Gorgonzola, cream cheese, and basil and pulse to combine. Using a rubber spatula, scrape the butter mixture onto a piece of plastic wrap and shape it into a log. Refrigerate until the log is firm.

When ready to cook the steaks, preheat the oven to 375°F. Heat a grill pan over high heat for 3 to 5 minutes. Drain the steaks and discard the marinade. Place the steaks in the grill pan and sear for 2 minutes. Turn the steaks and sear for 2 minutes more. Place the grill pan in the oven and roast the steaks for 8 to 10 minutes for medium-rare, or until an instant-read thermometer registers 120°F. Remove the steaks from the oven and let rest for 5 minutes.

Slice the Gorgonzola butter into ½-inch rounds and serve atop steaks.

dishin' with DAVID

BUTTERED UP

Compound butter, a fancy term for butter with added ingredients, is rolled into cylinders, wrapped in plastic, and then refrigerated or frozen until needed. Put a slice of flavored butter on burgers, grilled fish, baked or mashed potatoes, corn on the cob, and other vegetables.

meat loaf
with mashed potato topping

Meat loaf is a comfort-food classic, but I like it with a little French twist. This recipe offers what I love most about French onion soup—a gooey, cheesy layer and pronounced onion flavor. I top the meat loaf with creamy mashed potatoes and a savory brown gravy. This is a recipe sure to please the whole family.

MAKES 4 TO 6 SERVINGS

MEAT LOAF

2 pounds ground beef

1 medium onion, chopped

1 garlic clove, minced

½ envelope dry onion soup mix

2 large eggs

2 slices day-old white bread, torn into small pieces

2 teaspoons Worcestershire sauce

½ teaspoon freshly ground black pepper

GRAVY

1 tablespoon unsalted butter

¼ cup diced onion

1 tablespoon cornstarch

1 cup beef broth

1 teaspoon kosher salt

½ teaspoon freshly ground black pepper

Creamy Garlic Mashed Potatoes (page 107)

1 cup (4 ounces) grated Gruyère

Preheat the oven to 350°F.

To make the meat loaf, use your hands to combine the ground beef, onion, garlic, soup mix, eggs, bread, Worcestershire sauce, and pepper in a large bowl. For a tender meat loaf, don't overmix. Put the mixture in a 9 x 5 x 3-inch loaf pan. Bake for 1 hour. While the meat loaf is baking, make the gravy.

To make the gravy, melt the butter in a saucepan over medium heat. Add the onion and sauté until tender, about 5 minutes. Dissolve the cornstarch in 2 tablespoons water in a small dish and then add to the onion. Whisk in the beef broth and cook for 1 minute, until the gravy thickens. Whisk in the salt and pepper. Keep the gravy warm over low heat.

Remove the meat loaf from the oven and carefully drain off the liquid that has accumulated in the pan. Spread the mashed potatoes on top of the meat loaf and sprinkle on the Gruyère. Return the meat loaf to the oven and bake for 20 to 30 minutes more, until an instant-read thermometer inserted into the middle reads 165°F. Remove from the oven and let rest for 5 to 10 minutes before slicing. Serve with the warm gravy.

chicken-fried steak
with country gravy

I used to beg Mom to make this Southern classic whenever she had enough time on the weekends. Cube steak is tenderized, then dredged in flour, dipped in eggs, and fried. Seasonings are then added to the pan drippings to make a thicker-than-cream gravy. I can't imagine serving chicken-fried steak with anything but mashed potatoes, green beans, and biscuits to wipe my plate clean.

MAKES 2 TO 3 SERVINGS

STEAK

½ pound cube steak

½ teaspoon kosher salt

½ cup all-purpose flour

¼ cup bread crumbs

1 large egg

½ cup canola oil

COUNTRY GRAVY

1 tablespoon unsalted butter

3 tablespoons all-purpose flour

¼ teaspoon kosher salt

¼ teaspoon ground white pepper

½ teaspoon garlic powder

½ teaspoon onion powder

1½ cups milk, plus more if necessary

To make the steaks, cut the steak in half and place each half between two pieces of plastic wrap. Pound the steaks with a meat mallet to ¼-inch thickness and season with the salt.

Combine the flour and bread crumbs on a plate. On another plate, beat the egg with 2 teaspoons water. Dredge the steaks in the flour mixture, coat them with the egg mixture, then dredge them one more time in the flour mixture. Don't be gentle when pressing the flour mixture into the steaks. It has to adhere and form a crust during cooking.

Heat the canola oil in a large skillet. When the oil is hot, add the steaks and fry them until cooked through and golden brown, about 3 minutes per side. Transfer the steaks to a plate. Pour off all but 2 tablespoons of the oil from the skillet.

To make the gravy, melt the butter with the reserved oil in the skillet. Sprinkle the flour evenly over the skillet. Using a whisk, cook the roux until it is a deep golden brown. Whisk in the salt, white pepper, garlic powder, and onion powder. Slowly whisk in the milk and bring to a boil over medium heat. Continue for 8 to 10 minutes, stirring constantly, until the gravy has thickened. (Add a bit more milk if the gravy seems too thick.) Pour the gravy over the steaks before serving.

chicken-fried steak
with country gravy

I used to beg Mom to make this Southern classic whenever she had enough time on the week-ends. Cube steak is tenderized, then dredged in flour, dipped in eggs, and fried. Seasonings are then added to the pan drippings to make a thicker-than-cream gravy. I can't imagine serving chicken-fried steak with anything but mashed potatoes, green beans, and biscuits to wipe my plate clean.

MAKES 2 TO 3 SERVINGS

STEAK

½ pound cube steak

½ teaspoon kosher salt

½ cup all-purpose flour

¼ cup bread crumbs

1 large egg

½ cup canola oil

COUNTRY GRAVY

1 tablespoon unsalted butter

3 tablespoons all-purpose flour

¼ teaspoon kosher salt

¼ teaspoon ground white pepper

½ teaspoon garlic powder

½ teaspoon onion powder

1½ cups milk, plus more if necessary

To make the steaks, cut the steak in half and place each half between two pieces of plastic wrap. Pound the steaks with a meat mallet to ¼-inch thickness and season with the salt.

Combine the flour and bread crumbs on a plate. On another plate, beat the egg with 2 tea-spoons water. Dredge the steaks in the flour mixture, coat them with the egg mixture, then dredge them one more time in the flour mixture. Don't be gentle when pressing the flour mixture into the steaks. It has to adhere and form a crust during cooking.

Heat the canola oil in a large skillet. When the oil is hot, add the steaks and fry them until cooked through and golden brown, about 3 minutes per side. Transfer the steaks to a plate. Pour off all but 2 tablespoons of the oil from the skillet.

To make the gravy, melt the butter with the reserved oil in the skillet. Sprinkle the flour evenly over the skillet. Using a whisk, cook the roux until it is a deep golden brown. Whisk in the salt, white pepper, garlic powder, and onion powder. Slowly whisk in the milk and bring to a boil over medium heat. Continue for 8 to 10 minutes, stirring constantly, until the gravy has thickened. (Add a bit more milk if the gravy seems too thick.) Pour the gravy over the steaks before serving.

pot roast
with vegetables

Many Sunday mornings, Mom asked me to sear the meat for pot roast. Mom added the other ingredients and let the pot roast cook for hours. Oh my, how good the house smelled! The meat was fall-apart tender, and the gravy was thick and flavorful. As soon as there's a nip in the air, I begin to crave this dish and make it several times during the winter. Like Mom, I serve this with a basket of Mom's Mayonnaise Drop Biscuits (page 30).

MAKES 6 TO 8 SERVINGS

1 3- to 4-pound boneless bottom round roast
½ cup all-purpose flour
Kosher salt and freshly ground black pepper
¼ cup canola oil
2 medium onions, quartered
3 garlic cloves, smashed

1 tablespoon tomato paste
1 cup dry red wine
3 cups beef stock
2 fresh thyme sprigs
2 bay leaves
3 carrots, sliced into 1-inch pieces
6 Red Bliss potatoes, quartered
½ cup chopped fresh parsley

Preheat the oven to 350°F.

Pat the roast dry with paper towels. Spread the flour on a large plate. Dredge the roast in the flour, coating it completely. Season it liberally with salt and pepper.

Heat the canola oil in a Dutch oven over medium-high heat. Sear the meat on all sides until it is well browned. Remove the browned meat to a plate. Add the onions, garlic, and tomato paste to the pot and cook until the onions and garlic begin to turn golden. Add the red wine and cook, scraping up the browned bits from the bottom of the pot, until the wine has reduced to ½ cup, about 10 minutes. Return the meat to the pot.

Add the beef stock, thyme, and bay leaves and bring to a simmer. Cover and transfer to the oven. Roast for 2½ hours. Add the carrots and potatoes and roast for 2 hours more. Transfer the roast to a cutting board and let it rest for 15 to 20 minutes. While the meat is resting, skim the fat from the gravy. Transfer the gravy to a saucepan and heat. Cut the roast into thin slices, arrange them on a serving platter, and garnish with the parsley. Serve the pot roast accompanied by the gravy.

braised beef short ribs

Growing up in the South, we always ate pork, not beef, ribs. Once, when I walked into a friend's house, the warm aromas of herbs told me that something great was in the oven. When we sat down to dinner, I had my first taste of falling-off-the-bone beef short ribs. And I've been making them ever since. Serve short ribs on a bed of polenta, mashed potatoes, orzo, or with a loaf of crusty bread so you don't miss any of the robust gravy.

MAKES 4 TO 6 SERVINGS

¼ cup canola oil

½ cup all-purpose flour

Kosher salt and freshly ground black
    pepper

4½ pounds 3-inch-long bone-in beef
    short ribs

3 cups beef stock

1½ cups dry red wine

1 tablespoon tomato paste

½ cup finely chopped onion

3 garlic cloves, minced

2 carrots, coarsely chopped

2 fresh rosemary sprigs

2 fresh thyme sprigs

2 tablespoons unsalted butter

To make the short ribs, preheat the oven to 350°F.

Heat the canola oil in a large Dutch oven over medium heat. Combine the flour with a pinch of salt and pepper in a large dish. Dredge the short ribs in the flour mixture, shaking off any excess flour. Sear the short ribs in the hot oil until they are well browned on all sides. You may have to do this in batches. If so, remove the meat to a platter while browning the other meat.

Return all the meat to the pot. Add the beef stock, red wine, tomato paste, onion, garlic, carrots, rosemary, and thyme. There should be enough liquid to cover the ribs. If not, add water. Bring to a simmer. Cover the pot and transfer it to the oven. Braise until the liquid has reduced and the meat is falling off the bone, about 4 hours. (Check the pot halfway through cooking. If the meat looks dry, add a little more beef stock or water.)

Using tongs, transfer the ribs to a serving dish. Strain the cooking liquid and discard the solids. Return the cooking liquid to the pot, add the butter, and cook over low heat until the butter has melted and the mixture is heated through. Pour the sauce over the ribs and serve.

beef stew
with dumplings

Mention dumplings and most folks immediately think of chicken and dumplings. But why not top a pot of beef stew with some of those fluffy pillows of batter? In just ten minutes, this hearty stew becomes something really special.

MAKES 4 TO 6 SERVINGS

2 tablespoons canola oil

1 cup all-purpose flour

3 to 4 pounds beef chuck or bottom round, trimmed and cut into 1½-inch pieces

1 onion, chopped

1 baking potato, peeled and cut into 2-inch pieces

2 carrots, chopped

1 15-ounce can tomato sauce

5 cups beef stock

⅓ cup dry red wine

1 teaspoon kosher salt

¼ teaspoon freshly ground black pepper

1 10-ounce package frozen peas

2½ cups Bisquick

⅔ cups milk

½ cup chopped fresh parsley

Heat the canola oil in a Dutch oven over medium heat. Spread the flour on a shallow dish and dredge the meat in the flour. Add the meat to the pot, working in batches if necessary, and brown on all sides, 12 to 15 minutes, until a crust forms on the outside. Remove the meat to a platter while browning the remaining meat.

Return all the meat to the pot and add the onion, potato, carrots, tomato sauce, 1½ cups water, the beef stock, red wine, salt, and pepper. Bring to a boil, then reduce the heat, cover, and simmer for 1½ to 2 hours, until tender. Stir in the peas.

Stir the Bisquick and milk together in a bowl until a soft dough forms. Drop heaping table-spoons of the dough on top of the stew. Cook, covered, over low heat for 10 minutes. Ladle the stew and biscuits into warm bowls and sprinkle with parsley before serving.

dishin' with DAVID

AGAINST THE GRAIN

Cookbooks often tell you to slice meat "thinly against the grain," but what does that mean? Look at your brisket and you'll see lines in the meat that are parallel to one another. That's the grain. If you cut the meat on those lines, you'll end up with tough shreds, not tender slices. Slice the meat perpendicular to those lines for brisket perfection.

barbecued beef brisket

Brisket is a tough cut of meat that needs to cook a long time in the oven at a low temperature. Add some barbecue sauce and you've got a great spin on an old classic. Cook the brisket one day, refrigerate the meat to give the flavors time to develop, and then it can be easily sliced the next day. Leftovers make great sandwiches that you can enjoy with a side of Tangy Coleslaw (page 91).

No slow cooker? Cook the brisket in a 300°F oven until tender, 4 to 4½ hours.

MAKES 6 SERVINGS

DRY RUB

2 tablespoons kosher salt

1 teaspoon freshly ground black pepper

2 teaspoons paprika

1 teaspoon onion salt

2 teaspoons chili powder

1 teaspoon sugar

1 teaspoon ground celery seeds

1 teaspoon garlic powder

1 teaspoon dry mustard

1 teaspoon ground cumin

BRISKET

1 4- to 5-pound beef brisket

1 medium onion, sliced

2 garlic cloves, chopped

BARBECUE SAUCE

2 cups ketchup

1 cup Dijon mustard

½ cup Worcestershire sauce

¼ cup packed dark brown sugar

¼ cup molasses

1 tablespoon liquid smoke

To make the dry rub, combine the salt, pepper, paprika, onion salt, chili powder, sugar, celery seeds, garlic powder, dry mustard, and cumin in a small bowl. Rub the mixture evenly over both sides of the brisket. Place the brisket in a shallow dish, cover with aluminum foil, and refrigerate overnight.

Transfer the brisket to a slow cooker. Scatter the onion and garlic on top. Cover and cook on low until fork-tender, 6 to 8 hours. When the brisket is done, remove it to a cutting board and let it rest for 15 minutes before thinly slicing against the grain.

While the brisket is cooking, prepare the barbecue sauce. Combine the ketchup, mustard, Worcestershire sauce, brown sugar, molasses, and liquid smoke in a medium saucepan. Bring to a boil over medium-high heat, stirring occasionally. Remove the pan from the heat and allow the sauce to cool. Serve the sauce with the sliced brisket.

beef stroganoff
with buttered noodles

Named after a nineteenth-century Russian diplomat, beef Stroganoff was served at European-style, or "continental," restaurants in the 1950s. With strips of tender beef and plenty of mushrooms cooked in a sour cream–based sauce, serve this rich stew atop a pile of buttered noodles.

MAKES 4 TO 6 SERVINGS

2 tablespoons canola oil

1 2½-pound beef tenderloin, well trimmed, meat cut into 2 x 1 x ½-inch strips

6 tablespoons unsalted butter

¼ cup finely chopped shallots

1 pound small button mushrooms, sliced

Kosher salt and freshly ground black pepper

2 cups beef stock

2 tablespoons dry red wine

12 ounces wide egg noodles

2 tablespoons all-purpose flour

¾ cup heavy cream

½ cup (4 ounces) sour cream

1 tablespoon Dijon mustard

1 tablespoon chopped fresh dill

1 tablespoon paprika

Heat the canola oil in a large skillet over high heat until very hot. Pat the beef dry with paper towels. Working in batches, sear the beef just until brown on all sides. Transfer the beef to a platter.

Melt 2 tablespoons of the butter in the same skillet over medium-high heat. Add the shallots and sauté until they are softened, scraping up any browned bits from the bottom of the pan, about 2 minutes. Add the mushrooms, season with salt and pepper, and cook until the liquid evaporates, about 12 minutes. Add the beef stock and red wine. Simmer until the liquid thickens and just coats the mushrooms, 12 to 14 minutes.

Bring a large pot of salted water to a boil. Add the egg noodles and cook until tender, about 8 minutes. Remove ½ cup cooking liquid to a separate bowl. Drain the noodles and transfer to a bowl. Add the remaining 4 tablespoons butter and toss to coat. Season with salt and pepper.

Whisk the flour into the reserved cooking liquid until smooth. Pour the flour mixture into the skillet. Stir in the heavy cream, sour cream, and mustard. Add the beef and any accumulated juices. Simmer over medium-low heat until the beef is just heated through, about 2 minutes. Stir in the dill and season with salt and pepper.

Divide the noodles among plates and top with the beef and sauce. Sprinkle with paprika and serve.

bolognese sauce
with pappardelle

I still remember the first time I saw this dish on a menu and asked the waiter to describe it. He went into a long description—how the sauce made with three kinds of meat was slowly simmered, how the carrots melted into the sauce, and how milk, the secret ingredient, added smoothness. He then added that the savory sauce was served on a bed of pasta called pappardelle. While pappardelle, wide flat noodles similar to fettuccine, are the traditional accompaniment, any pasta works with this rich, meaty sauce.

MAKES 4 SERVINGS

2 tablespoons extra virgin olive oil
2 tablespoons unsalted butter
1 small onion, finely diced
1 carrot, finely diced
1 celery stalk, finely diced
½ pound ground beef chuck
½ pound ground pork
½ pound ground veal

Kosher salt and freshly ground black
　pepper
1 cup dry white wine
1 cup milk
Pinch of ground nutmeg
1 28-ounce can tomato puree
1 pound pappardelle or other pasta
½ cup freshly grated Parmigiano-Reggiano

Heat the olive oil and butter in a Dutch oven over moderately high heat until the foaming subsides. Add the onion, carrot, and celery and sauté until the vegetables soften, 3 to 4 minutes. Add the ground beef, pork, and veal and cook, stirring, until the meat is no longer pink, about 2 minutes. Season with salt and pepper. Add the white wine and cook, stirring occasionally, until most of the wine has evaporated, about 10 minutes. Add the milk and nutmeg and cook, stirring occasionally, until the liquid has evaporated, about 10 minutes.

Stir the pureed tomatoes into the sauce and bring to a simmer. Simmer, uncovered, stirring occasionally, until the sauce is thickened and the flavors are blended, about 1½ hours.

Bring a large pot of salted water to a boil. Add the pappardelle and cook until tender but still firm to the bite. Drain the pasta and divide it among warm bowls. Ladle on the sauce and toss with the pasta. Serve immediately with the Parmigiano-Reggiano.

dishin' with
DAVID

TABLE TALK

Every time chef, author, and television host Lidia Bastianich appears on the show, I learn so many new things about Italian food. But there's one thing she shared that we both agree on: "The best part of a meal is sitting around the table with the friends and family you love. A meal should take time. Don't rush the dessert. After the meal, clear the table, clean up, and let people just do their thing. Then, bring the dessert. It's important to have an interlude there. I like to serve my dessert family style so everyone can help themselves."

old world spaghetti and meatballs

A bowl of spaghetti with homemade sauce, some meatballs, and a sprinkle of Parmesan is my idea of comfort.

MAKES 6 SERVINGS

SAUCE

2 tablespoons extra virgin olive oil

½ yellow onion, chopped

3 garlic cloves, chopped

2 28-ounce cans Italian plum tomatoes

¼ cup chopped fresh basil

¼ cup chopped fresh parsley

¼ cup dry red wine

1 teaspoon kosher salt, or to taste

MEATBALLS

¾ cup fresh bread cubes

2 large eggs

1 onion, grated

½ cup milk

½ cup freshly grated Pecorino Romano

2 tablespoons finely chopped fresh basil

2 tablespoons finely chopped fresh parsley

2 teaspoons kosher salt

2 teaspoons freshly ground black pepper

2 pounds mixed ground beef, pork, and veal

1 tablespoon extra virgin olive oil

1½ pounds spaghetti or other long, thin pasta

¼ cup freshly grated Pecorino Romano

To make the sauce, heat the olive oil in a large Dutch oven over medium-high heat. Add the onion and cook until it is beginning to soften, about 2 minutes. Add the garlic and cook for 1 minute. Add the tomatoes and their juices, the basil, and parsley, and stir to combine. Using a potato masher, gently crush the tomatoes and continue to cook until the sauce begins to thicken, about 5 minutes. Stir in the red wine and return the sauce to a boil. Reduce the heat to a simmer and season the sauce with salt to taste. Simmer the sauce while preparing the meatballs.

To make the meatballs, combine the bread cubes, eggs, onion, milk, pecorino, basil, parsley, salt, and pepper in a large bowl. Using your hands, add the meat mixture and mix until just combined. Be careful not to overwork or the meatballs will be tough. Form the mixture into 2-inch balls.

Heat the olive oil in a large frying pan over high heat. Working in batches, brown the meatballs on all sides, 2 to 3 minutes per batch. Transfer the meatballs to the pot with the sauce and simmer until the meatballs are cooked through and the sauce is thick, 30 to 45 minutes. (Alternatively, bake the meatballs in a 325°F oven until they are cooked through, about 30 minutes.)

While the sauce is simmering, bring a large pot of salted water to a boil. Add the spaghetti and cook until it is al dente, tender but still firm to the bite, 8 to 10 minutes.

To serve, spread a thin layer of sauce on each plate. Top with pasta, more sauce, and meatballs and sprinkle with the Pecorino.

sloppy joes

Mom often made sloppy Joes when she wanted to have a quick weeknight dinner. Eating sloppy Joes is a messy matter, but frankly, that's part of the fun. There's no way you can eat one and keep it from falling apart, so Mom put extra toasted buns on the table so we could wipe our plates clean.

MAKES 6 SERVINGS

1 tablespoon extra virgin olive oil
½ cup shredded carrots
1 medium onion, finely chopped
1 celery stalk, finely chopped
1 jalapeño, stemmed, seeded, and diced
2 garlic cloves, minced
½ teaspoon kosher salt
2 pounds ground beef
2 cups tomato sauce
½ cup ketchup

1 tablespoon Worcestershire sauce
1 tablespoon red wine vinegar
1 teaspoon hot sauce
2 tablespoons dark brown sugar
½ teaspoon dried thyme
Pinch of ground cloves
Pinch of cayenne
Pinch of freshly ground black pepper

6 hamburger buns

Heat the olive oil in a large sauté pan over medium-high heat. Add the carrots and sauté until tender, about 5 minutes. Add the onion, celery, and jalapeño and cook until the onion is translucent, about 5 minutes. Add the garlic and cook for 30 seconds. Transfer the vegetables to a medium bowl and set aside.

Sprinkle the bottom of the pan with the salt and heat it over high heat. Working in batches, crumble the beef into the pan and let it cook undisturbed until the bottom is well browned. Flip and continue to cook until well browned. Using a slotted spoon, transfer the beef to the bowl with the vegetables.

Drain off all but 1 tablespoon of fat from the pan. Return the beef-vegetable mixture to the pan and stir in the tomato sauce, ketchup, Worcestershire sauce, vinegar, hot sauce, brown sugar, thyme, cloves, cayenne, and black pepper. Bring the mixture to a simmer and cook until the beef is cooked through, about 10 minutes. Taste and adjust the seasonings. Divide the mixture among the bottom halves of the buns. Cover with the top halves and serve.

french dip roast beef sandwiches

Whenever I go out to lunch, I scan the menu, and once I see that the restaurant offers a French dip, I read no further. It is my go-to sandwich. Some slowly cooked, thinly sliced roast beef is piled on a roll and accompanied with a small bowl of the meat's natural juices (*jus* in French) for dipping. The meat is topped with cheese, and the sandwich is served with some crunchy potato chips and coleslaw. When I finish my sandwich, I dip any leftover chips in any remaining juices. I make these with leftover roast beef or beef I buy at the deli counter.

MAKES 6 SERVINGS

SAUCE

2 tablespoons unsalted butter

1 shallot, minced

1 tablespoon all-purpose flour

¼ cup dry sherry

1 teaspoon McCormick's Montreal Steak Seasoning

1 tablespoon Better Than Bouillon Beef Base

SANDWICHES

8 ounces thinly sliced Swiss or provolone cheese

6 French bread rolls, halved

1 pound sliced rare roast beef

Preheat the broiler.

To make the sauce, melt the butter in a saucepan over medium heat. Add the shallot and sauté until translucent. Whisk in the flour and stir for 1 minute. Whisk in the sherry and steak seasoning and cook for 1 to 2 minutes. Dissolve the beef base in 2 cups boiling water, then slowly whisk the mixture into the saucepan. Bring the sauce to a simmer and cook for 2 to 4 minutes. Using a fine-mesh strainer, strain the sauce into a bowl. Discard the solids in the strainer. Return the sauce to the saucepan and keep warm over low heat while preparing the sandwiches.

To make the sandwiches, divide the cheese among 6 roll halves. Place the halves with the cheese on a baking sheet and put under the broiler, just until the cheese melts, about 1 minute.

Place the roast beef on top of the cheese. Return the halves to the broiler to heat the roast beef, about 1 minute. Put the tops on the sandwiches and pass a pitcher of the warm sauce when serving.

seafood
jump right in

FOR FRESHNESS OF flavor and simplicity of preparation, it's hard to beat seafood. From the rich taste of salmon to the mild flakiness of tilapia to the sweetness of shrimp, fish and shellfish are so versatile. They can be steamed, sautéed, fried, grilled, or baked.

Only your imagination limits what goes with your seafood. For example, roasted tilapia or grilled salmon can be served with a vibrant salsa, a white wine pan sauce, lemon and capers, an herbal mayonnaise, or a mustardy cream sauce. If you want the fresh, simple flavors of fish and shellfish to come through, all you need is a squeeze of fresh lemon. Any green vegetable, some pasta, or a scoop of rice is the perfect side dishes.

After reading all the recipes in this chapter, you'll wonder why you aren't eating fish and shellfish more often.

fried calamari
with marinara sauce

This appetizer is so popular that it's on menus everywhere from diners to high-end restaurants. Now, there's no reason to get all squeamish when you learn that *calamari* is the Italian word for "squid." These days calamari are available cleaned, fresh or frozen, and even cut up into rings. All you have to do is coat them in buttermilk, dredge them in flour, and fry them until crispy. A bowl of warm marinara sauce and some lemon wedges are the traditional accompaniments.

MAKES 4 TO 6 SERVINGS

MARINARA SAUCE

2 tablespoons extra virgin olive oil

1 large onion, diced

1 teaspoon kosher salt

3 garlic cloves, minced

1 28-ounce can crushed tomatoes

1 28-ounce can tomato puree

½ teaspoon sugar

1 teaspoon onion powder

2 teaspoons dried Italian seasoning

½ cup freshly grated Parmigiano-Reggiano

CALAMARI

1 pound calamari, cleaned and sliced into ¼-inch rings

1 cup buttermilk

1 cup all-purpose flour

1 cup cornmeal

1 teaspoon kosher salt

¼ teaspoon freshly ground black pepper

¼ teaspoon cayenne

Canola oil for frying

To make the sauce, heat the olive oil in a large saucepan over medium heat. Add the onion and salt and sauté until soft, 5 to 7 minutes. Add the garlic and continue cooking for 1 to 2 minutes. Add the crushed tomatoes and tomato puree and stir to combine. Add the sugar, onion powder, Italian seasoning, and Parmigiano-Reggiano. Reduce the heat and simmer until the sauce has thickened, 30 to 40 minutes.

To make the calamari, rinse the calamari under cold running water and pat dry with paper towels. Combine the buttermilk and ¼ cup water in a large bowl. Add the calamari and toss to coat. Combine the flour, cornmeal, salt, black pepper, and cayenne in a shallow bowl and whisk to blend. Drain the calamari and add to the bowl with the flour-cornmeal mixture. Toss until they are evenly coated.

Pour 3 inches of canola oil into a saucepan and heat over medium-high heat. Dip a piece of the calamari in the oil to test if the oil is hot enough. If it sizzles, the oil is ready. Reduce the heat to medium. Working in batches, fry the calamari for 1 minute. Turn over the pieces and continue to fry until they are lightly golden brown, about 1 minute. Be careful not to overcook or the calamari will be rubbery. Transfer the calamari to paper towels to drain. Serve hot with the marinara sauce.

herb-encrusted tilapia

If some folks in your family are a little unsure about eating fish, then tilapia is a good introduction. Talapia is mild, white, flaky, and moist. A quick soak in some buttermilk, adding fresh herbs to crunchy bread crumbs, and baking the fish at a high temperature will surprise those who might be tempted to veer away. If there's no tilapia in the market, you can substitute flounder or catfish fillets. Serve on a bed of Israeli Couscous with Peas, Asparagus, and Mint (page 104).

MAKES 4 SERVINGS

½ cup buttermilk

½ teaspoon kosher salt

¼ teaspoon freshly ground black pepper

4 6- to 8-ounce tilapia fillets

Vegetable cooking spray

½ cup bread crumbs

½ cup panko (Japanese bread crumbs)

2 teaspoons minced fresh parsley

2 teaspoons minced fresh basil

2 teaspoons minced fresh chives

2 teaspoons finely grated lemon zest

Whisk together the buttermilk, salt, and pepper in a shallow dish large enough to hold the fish in a single layer. Add the tilapia and turn to coat. Cover and refrigerate for 1 hour.

Place an oven rack in the top third of the oven. Preheat the oven to 425°F. Line a baking sheet with aluminum foil. Place a wire rack on the prepared baking sheet and spray the wire rack with the vegetable cooking spray.

Combine the bread crumbs, panko, parsley, basil, chives, and lemon zest on a shallow plate.

Drain the buttermilk from the tilapia and dredge each fillet in the bread crumb mixture. Arrange the tilapia on the prepared wire rack. Bake until the coating is crisp and golden brown and the fish is opaque in the center, 12 to 15 minutes.

crispy fish and chips

On my first visit to London, I can remember walking down the quaint streets and suddenly smelling vinegar and something fried. I looked around for a restaurant but couldn't see one. Instead, a man behind me was enjoying vinegar-doused fish and chips wrapped in a cone made from newspaper. In the United Kingdom, fish and chip joints can be found in every neighborhood. Here, it's easy to make fish and chips at home. A light crispy coating keeps the fish moist and tender.

MAKES 6 SERVINGS

4 large baking potatoes
1 cup plus ½ cup all-purpose flour
½ teaspoon baking powder
½ teaspoon baking soda
1 teaspoon kosher salt
¼ teaspoon cayenne

1 12-ounce bottle beer
4 to 6 cups canola oil for frying
1½ pounds firm-fleshed whitefish (tilapia, pollock, cod) fillets, cut into serving-size pieces
Malt vinegar

Preheat the oven to 200°F. Line two baking sheets with parchment paper and set a wire rack over each one.

Leaving the skins on, slice the potatoes lengthwise into ½-inch strips. Place the potatoes in a bowl and cover with cold water.

Whisk together the 1 cup flour, the baking powder, baking soda, salt, and cayenne in a bowl. Whisk in the beer until the batter is completely smooth and free of any lumps. Refrigerate for 15 minutes. (The batter can be made up to 1 hour ahead of time.)

Clip a deep-frying thermometer to the side of a heavy, deep pot. Add the canola oil to the pot and slowly heat the oil to 325°F. Put the remaining ½ cup flour on a shallow plate.

Drain the potatoes and dry them thoroughly to remove any excess water. (A salad spinner works well.) Working in small batches, add some of the potatoes to the hot oil and fry for 2 to 3 minutes, just until pale and floppy. Using a slotted spoon, remove the potatoes from the oil and drain on one of the wire racks. When all the potatoes are fried, raise the heat and increase the temperature of the oil to 375°F. Return the potatoes to the oil and cook until brown and crisp, 2 to 3 minutes. Transfer the potatoes to the lined baking sheets and put them in the oven while you cook the fish.

Lower the heat and decrease the temperature of the oil to 350°F. Remove the batter from the refrigerator. Line a baking sheet with paper towels and set a roasting rack on top.

Lightly dredge the fish strips in the flour. Working in small batches, dip the fish into the batter and immerse in the hot oil. When the batter is set, turn over the pieces of fish and cook until golden brown, about 2 minutes. Drain on the roasting rack. Continue cooking the remaining pieces of fish. Serve the hot fish and the chips with malt vinegar on the side.

linguine
with scallops and shrimp in white wine cream sauce

Here's an elegant pull-out-all-the-stops entrée to serve at celebrations or special dinner parties. Top it off with some freshly grated Parmesan and chopped fresh parsley for a pop of color.

MAKES 4 TO 6 SERVINGS

¼ cup plus 2 tablespoons extra virgin olive oil

3 shallots, chopped

4 garlic cloves, minced

2 cups dry white wine

2 tablespoons chopped fresh parsley plus ¼ cup for garnish

2 teaspoons chopped fresh tarragon

1 teaspoon chopped fresh thyme

1 cup heavy cream

1 tablespoon fresh lemon juice

1 pound sea scallops

¾ pound large shrimp, peeled and deveined

1 teaspoon kosher salt

1 teaspoon freshly ground black pepper

1 pound linguine

½ cup freshly grated Parmigiano-Reggiano

Heat ¼ cup of the olive oil in a large sauté pan over medium heat. Add the shallots and garlic and sauté until translucent, about 2 minutes. Whisk in the white wine, 2 tablespoons parsley, tarragon, and thyme and cook until the mixture has reduced by half, 5 to 8 minutes. Reduce the heat to low, add the cream and lemon juice, and cook until the sauce has thickened, 3 to 5 minutes.

Sprinkle the scallops and shrimp with the salt and pepper. Heat the remaining 2 tablespoons olive oil in a large skillet over medium-high heat. Add the scallops and sauté just until they are opaque. Transfer to a platter and cover to keep warm. Add the shrimp to the skillet and sauté just until pink. Transfer them to the platter with the scallops.

Bring a large pot of water to a boil. Add the linguine and cook until tender but still firm to the bite. Drain the pasta and add it to the skillet. Top with the cream sauce, scallops, and shrimp (reserve a few scallops and shrimp for garnish). Toss to combine. Transfer the pasta to a serving platter and sprinkle with the Parmesan. Arrange the reserved scallops and shrimp over the top and sprinkle with the remaining parsley.

grilled salmon
with sour cream–dill sauce

It makes sense that salmon is such a popular fish. It's readily available, cooks quickly, goes well with all kinds of herbs and spices, and can be made on an outdoor grill or on top of the stove. The dish is made complete with a creamy sauce and a little dill. Pair salmon with some steamed asparagus or snap peas garnished with chopped scallions.

MAKES 4 SERVINGS

DILL SAUCE

⅓ cup (about 3 ounces) sour cream

⅓ cup mayonnaise

1 tablespoon minced shallot

½ teaspoon finely grated lemon zest

Juice of ½ lemon

2 teaspoons chopped fresh dill

¼ teaspoon sugar

¼ teaspoon garlic powder

1 teaspoon kosher salt

½ teaspoon freshly ground black pepper

SALMON

Vegetable oil spray

2 tablespoons unsalted butter, at room temperature

Fresh dill sprigs

Lemon slices

4 6-ounce salmon fillets

1 teaspoon lemon pepper seasoning

1 teaspoon kosher salt

To make the sauce, whisk together the sour cream, mayonnaise, shallot, lemon zest, lemon juice, dill, sugar, garlic powder, salt, and pepper in a small bowl. Set aside.

To grill the salmon, preheat a grill pan over high heat for 2 to 3 minutes. Spray the grill pan with the vegetable oil spray. Spread the butter on the belly side of each salmon fillet and season both sides with the lemon pepper seasoning and salt. Grill the salmon for 4 to 5 minutes on each side, turning them just once, until no longer pink inside. Divide the salmon among four plates. Top each fillet with some dill sauce. Garnish with fresh dill sprigs and lemon slices before serving.

make it your own

Instead of the dill sauce, try

* a pat of compound butter (page 181) on top of each serving
* pesto
* salsa
* add some chopped cucumber to the dill sauce
* chopped avocado and red onion
* artichoke hearts
* roasted red peppers
* yogurt in place of sour cream

low-country boil

Head down to coastal North and South Carolina and you'll always find people having low-country boils on the beach. When I was in college, my friends and I would head to the beach, build a fire pit, and cook up some seafood, sausage, and corn. Whether you have a low-country boil on the beach or in your backyard, you'll need the biggest pot you can find, preferably one with a basket insert. There's something here for everyone—crabs and shrimp for seafood lovers, sausage for landlubbers, and corn on the cob and potatoes for all. If you can't locate crabs, double up on the shrimp. Once everything is cooked, the liquid is drained off (here's where the insert basket comes in handy) and the crab, shrimp, sausage, and vegetables are spilled out onto newspaper-lined picnic tables. Let's eat!

MAKES 6 TO 8 SERVINGS

4 pounds small red potatoes

2 12-ounce cans beer

3 tablespoons Old Bay Seasoning

5 pounds snow or king crabs, broken into pieces

2 pounds kielbasa or other smoked sausage, sliced crosswise into 2-inch pieces

6 to 8 fresh ears of corn, halved

4 pounds large shrimp, peeled and deveined

Melted butter

Cocktail sauce

Put the potatoes in a large, deep pot and cover with 4 quarts water. Add the beer and Old Bay Seasoning, cover, and bring to a rolling boil. Boil for 5 minutes. Add the crabs, kielbasa, and corn and return to a boil. Boil until the potatoes are tender and can be pierced easily with a knife, about 10 minutes. Add the shrimp and boil until they are just cooked through, 3 to 4 minutes.

Carefully drain the pot and spread the contents on a picnic table covered with newspaper. Serve with the melted butter and cocktail sauce.

crab cakes

Crab cakes can be served in a variety of ways. Put a crab cake on top of a salad. Make smaller ones to pass as appetizers at a cocktail party. Try a crab cake po'boy on a roll with some mayonnaise, lettuce, and tomato. Shape the mixture into one-inch crab balls and bake. Serve as an elegant dinner entrée with steamed mixed vegetables and oven-roasted new potatoes.

MAKES 4 LARGE OR 6 MEDIUM CAKES

CAPER SAUCE

1 cup mayonnaise
½ cup capers, drained and coarsely
    chopped
2 tablespoons extra virgin olive oil
1 tablespoon Dijon mustard

1 tablespoon chopped fresh parsley
1 teaspoon fresh lemon juice
1 teaspoon Old Bay Seasoning
Dash of hot sauce

CRAB CAKES

1 cup heavy cream
1 tablespoon Worcestershire sauce
¼ to ½ teaspoon hot sauce, as desired
4 slices day-old Italian bread, crusts
    removed, bread cubed
¼ cup chopped fresh parsley
2 teaspoons Old Bay Seasoning
½ teaspoon dry mustard

¼ teaspoon cayenne
1 large egg, lightly beaten
1½ pounds jumbo lump crabmeat, picked
    over to remove any shells
½ cup or more canola oil
2 to 3 tablespoons unsalted butter
Lemon wedges

To make the caper sauce, whisk together the mayonnaise, capers, olive oil, mustard, parsley, lemon juice, Old Bay Seasoning, and hot sauce in a medium bowl. Cover and refrigerate. (The sauce can be made up to 2 days ahead.)

To make the crab cakes, combine the cream, Worcestershire sauce, and hot sauce in a medium sauté pan. Bring to a boil over medium-high heat and add the bread cubes. Stir to combine and remove from the heat. Allow the mixture to cool.

Whisk together the parsley, Old Bay Seasoning, mustard, and cayenne in a large bowl. Whisk in the beaten egg. Add the crabmeat and half of the bread mixture. Mix gently with a spatula just until combined. Add the remaining bread mixture in small increments, just until the crab mixture holds together (you may not need all the bread mixture). Be careful not to overmix. Form the crab mixture into 4 large or 6 medium cakes. Transfer the cakes to a parchment-lined baking sheet. Refrigerate for 1 hour.

Preheat the oven to 350°F.

Heat 2 tablespoons of the canola oil and 1 tablespoon of the butter in a large skillet over medium heat. When the butter starts to foam, add 2 or 3 crab cakes to the skillet and cook until golden brown, 2 to 3 minutes per side. Transfer the crab cakes to paper towels to drain. Add more oil and butter to the skillet and repeat with the remaining crab cakes.

Transfer the crab cakes back to the parchment-lined baking sheet. Bake for 15 minutes, until cooked through. Serve with the caper sauce and lemon wedges.

shrimp and cheesy grits

Go to a Southern grocery store and you'll find grits front and center. When I moved to the North, I always had to ask where the grits were in the market. Once I found them, there were just a few dusty boxes on a bottom shelf. Shrimp and grits, an especially popular dish in the coastal areas of the South where shrimp is plentiful, is quickly gaining popularity across the country. As a result, grits are now more widely available.

People sometimes complain that grits are too bland, but not in this dish. Cheese, scallions, and shrimp add plenty of flavors. This recipe is a rib-sticking classic that can be served at any meal.

MAKES 4 TO 6 SERVINGS

2 bacon slices, cooked (page 137) and crumbled; drippings reserved

2 cups milk

1 teaspoon kosher salt

1 cup stone-ground grits

2 cups (8 ounces) shredded Cheddar

½ cup (4 ounces) sour cream

1 tablespoon unsalted butter

¼ cup chopped scallions

1 teaspoon freshly ground black pepper

1 tablespoon extra virgin olive oil

1½ pounds large shrimp, peeled and deveined

4 teaspoons fresh lemon juice

2 garlic cloves, minced

2 tablespoons chopped fresh parsley

Preheat the oven to 350°F.

Heat the bacon drippings in a skillet over medium heat. Add 2 cups water, the milk, and salt. Bring the mixture to a boil and add the grits. Cook, stirring constantly, until all the liquid is absorbed, 20 to 25 minutes. Stir in the Cheddar, sour cream, butter, scallions, and pepper until the cheese melts.

While the grits are cooking, heat the olive oil in a large skillet over medium-high heat. Add the shrimp and sauté until they turn pink, about 3 minutes. Do not overcook. Add the lemon juice and garlic. Remove the skillet from the heat.

Divide the grits among bowls. Top with the shrimp mixture and garnish with the crumbled bacon and parsley.

shrimp po'boy

"Do you want that dressed?" they'll ask you when you order a po'boy in New Orleans. "Dressed" means that the crusty French bread roll is spread with mayonnaise, lettuce, and tomato. I like to spice up my dressing by adding some bold flavors to the mayonnaise. Be creative. To use a phrase I like, "Be fearless." Add some more heat if you like and throw on a few fried oysters.

MAKES 4 SERVINGS

ZESTY MAYONNAISE

¾ cup mayonnaise

1 garlic clove, minced

2 scallions, thinly sliced

1 tablespoon chopped fresh parsley

2 teaspoons capers, drained and chopped

2 teaspoons coarse-grain mustard

1 teaspoon red wine vinegar

½ teaspoon kosher salt

½ teaspoon freshly ground black pepper

¼ teaspoon hot sauce

SHRIMP

1 teaspoon garlic powder

1 teaspoon paprika

½ teaspoon dried oregano

½ teaspoon dried thyme

½ teaspoon onion powder

1 pound medium shrimp, peeled and deveined

Canola oil for frying

1 large egg

1 cup milk

1 cup all-purpose flour

4 French rolls

Shredded iceberg lettuce

Sliced tomatoes

To make the zesty mayonnaise, whisk together the mayonnaise, garlic, scallions, parsley, capers, mustard, vinegar, salt, pepper, and hot sauce in a medium bowl. Cover and refrigerate while making the shrimp.

To make the shrimp, combine the garlic powder, paprika, oregano, thyme, and onion powder in a large bowl. Add the shrimp and toss to coat.

Clip a deep-frying thermometer to the side of a heavy, deep pot. Add 2 inches of canola oil and heat to 350°F.

Beat the egg and milk together in a bowl. Put the flour on a shallow plate. Working in batches, dip the shrimp in the egg mixture and then coat them with the flour, shaking off any excess. Using a slotted spoon, lower the shrimp—not too many at a time—into the hot oil and fry until golden brown, about 4 minutes. When they are crisp and brown, transfer the cooked shrimp to a wire rack set over paper towels to drain. Cook the remaining shrimp.

Spread the French rolls with the spicy mayonnaise. Divide the shrimp among the rolls and top the shrimp with the lettuce and tomatoes, if desired.

desserts
sweet, sweet gratification

FOR THOSE OF us who come from the South, a piece of seasonal pie or cobbler, a slice of triple layer cake, or a bowl of smooth banana pudding was expected and served at the end of every meal. And believe me, I ate them all. These days I tend to save desserts for the finish of special meals at home or while eating out.

In my family, my grandmothers and mom were each known for their individual specialties. Both grandmothers made the best tender and flaky pies and cobblers with all kinds of seasonal fruit fillings. Mom was the cookie and cake baker. Her recipes came from everyone and everywhere. I remember that she had a plastic file box bulging with recipes handwritten on index cards and torn from magazines or peeled off cans. And most of them were for desserts. At Christmastime, Mom baked dozens of different kinds of cookies. I was her helper—measuring ingredients and shelling endless piles of nuts.

Encourage your kids to make desserts with you. There's something magical when it comes time to put all the ingredients together and you end up with something homemade and sweetly gratifying.

deep-dish apple pie

If I absolutely had to choose one category of dessert as my favorite, it would certainly be pie. As a child, when my birthday rolled around, I often asked for apple pie—with candles—instead of a traditional layer cake with frosting. Because a regular two-crust pie with apples is so good, then why not have a mile-high deep-dish pie with more crust and even more layers of apples? And I prefer to eat my pie at room temperature the day after it's baked. There's just something about how all those flavors come together once they've had a chance to sit for a while.

MAKES 8 SERVINGS

CRUST

2½ cups all-purpose flour

1 teaspoon granulated sugar

¼ teaspoon kosher salt

½ pound (2 sticks) cold unsalted butter, diced

¼ cup cold vegetable shortening, diced

2 large egg yolks

FILLING

2 pounds Granny Smith apples, peeled, cored, and cut into medium slices

1 pound Cortland apples, peeled, cored, and cut into medium slices

Juice of 1 large lemon

⅓ cup packed light brown sugar

⅓ cup packed dark brown sugar

¼ cup granulated sugar

3 tablespoons cornstarch

2 teaspoons ground cinnamon

¼ teaspoon ground nutmeg

¼ teaspoon kosher salt

1 tablespoon cold unsalted butter, diced

EGG WASH

1 large egg yolk

1 tablespoon heavy cream

1 tablespoon granulated sugar

To make the crust, place the flour, granulated sugar, and salt in a food processor and pulse to combine. Gradually add the butter and shortening and pulse until incorporated and the mixture resembles coarse meal. In a small bowl, whisk the egg yolks with 6 tablespoons ice water. Drizzle the egg yolk mixture into the food processor and pulse until the dough comes together in a ball. Be careful not to overmix.

Turn the dough out onto a floured work surface and divide it in half. Flatten each half into a disk, wrap in plastic wrap, and chill in the refrigerator for 1 hour.

To make the filling, put the apple slices in a large bowl and toss with the lemon juice. In a small bowl, combine the light brown sugar, dark brown sugar, granulated sugar, cornstarch, cinnamon, nutmeg, and salt and stir with a fork until no lumps remain. Stir the sugar mixture into the apple mixture.

On a lightly floured work surface, roll out one piece of dough into a 12-inch circle about ⅛ inch thick. Gently ease the dough into a 10 x 2-inch deep-dish pie plate. Using a paring knife, trim to the edge of the pie plate. Transfer the crust to the freezer and freeze until firm, about 30 minutes.

To make the egg wash, whisk the egg yolk and cream together in a small bowl.

Remove the pie shell from the freezer and fill with the apple mixture. Dot with the tablespoon of diced butter. Brush the edges of the dough with the egg wash.

On a lightly floured work surface, roll out the second piece of dough into a 14-inch circle. Carefully drape it over the pie and crimp the edges. (Cut off any excess dough.) Brush the top of the pie with the remaining egg wash. Freeze or refrigerate the pie until firm, at least 30 minutes. Using a knife, make 3 to 4 slits in the top to let steam escape. Sprinkle with the sugar.

Preheat the oven to 400°F.

Place the pie on a baking sheet and bake until the crust is just beginning to brown, about 20 minutes. Reduce the oven temperature to 350°F and continue to bake until the crust is golden brown and the juices are bubbling, 35 to 45 minutes. (If the crust begins to get too dark, drape a piece of aluminum foil over the surface.) Cool the pie on a wire rack before serving.

southern pecan pie

When I was growing up in the South, many of my friends and family members had pecan trees and often brought us bags of nuts. Mom kept a big bowl of pecans and a nutcracker by the hearth so we could snack on the nuts. We ate pecan pie at our house, at other people's homes, and at church suppers. I, however, had my own special way of eating my slice. First, I'd peel off and eat the top layer of nuts. Then I savored the sweet, gooey filling, leaving the flaky crust for last.

MAKES 8 SERVINGS

PIECRUST

1¼ cups all-purpose flour, plus extra for
    rolling
½ teaspoon kosher salt

½ teaspoon granulated sugar
8 tablespoons (1 stick) cold unsalted
    butter, diced

FILLING

1 cup packed light brown sugar
1 cup dark corn syrup
2 tablespoons unsalted butter, melted
3 large eggs

1 teaspoon pure vanilla extract
¼ teaspoon kosher salt
2 cups pecan halves (about 9½ ounces),
    toasted

TOPPING

1 cup chilled heavy cream

2 tablespoons granulated sugar

To make the piecrust, place the flour, salt, and granulated sugar in a food processor and pulse 3 or 4 times to mix. Add the butter to the flour mixture through the feed tube. Pulse 6 to 8 times, until the mixture resembles coarse meal. With the machine running, add 3 tablespoons ice water, pulsing until the mixture just holds together. If necessary, add 1 or 2 tablespoons ice water.

Remove the dough from the machine. Press it together into a ball and then flatten it into a small disk. Wrap the dough in plastic wrap and refrigerate for 1 hour.

Roll out the dough on a lightly floured work surface to a 13-inch round. Transfer to a 9-inch pie plate. Trim the edges, leaving a ½-inch overhang. Fold under the overhang and crimp the edges decoratively. Refrigerate the crust until firm, about 1 hour.

Preheat the oven to 375°F.

Line the piecrust with buttered aluminum foil and fill with dried beans or pie weights. Bake the crust until the edges begin to brown, about 7 minutes. Remove the foil and beans. Continue baking until the bottom of the crust is golden brown, about 5 minutes more. If the crust bubbles, press it back into shape with a fork. Cool the crust on a wire rack. Leave the oven on.

To make the filling, whisk together the brown sugar, corn syrup, and butter in a bowl until blended. Whisk in the eggs, one at a time. Stir in the vanilla and salt. Fold in the pecans. Pour the filling into the crust and bake until the edges are puffed and the center is just set, about 50 minutes. Cool the pie on a wire rack for at least 30 minutes.

To make the topping, beat the cream and granulated sugar in the bowl of an electric mixer until soft peaks form. Slice the pie and serve with a spoonful of whipped cream.

chocolate–peanut butter pie

Once I tasted that famous chocolate–peanut butter cup, I was hooked on the combination. This pie brings both flavors together in a creamy, mouthwatering way. Top it off with some whipped cream, and you'll have "Yum! Yum! faces" all around the table.

MAKES 8 SERVINGS

1 9-inch prepared graham cracker piecrust

FILLING

1 cup (6 ounces) semisweet chocolate chips

¾ cup heavy cream

1 8-ounce package cream cheese, softened (do not use nonfat cream cheese)

1 cup chunky peanut butter

½ cup granulated sugar

2 teaspoons pure vanilla extract

TOPPING

1 cup heavy cream

2 tablespoons confectioners' sugar

½ teaspoon pure vanilla extract

Grated or shaved semisweet chocolate

Unsalted peanuts

Preheat the oven to 375°F.

Bake the graham cracker piecrust for 7 to 8 minutes. Cool completely on a wire rack.

To make the filling, combine the chocolate chips and cream in a microwave-safe bowl. Microwave on high in 20-second intervals until the chocolate is melted. Stir thoroughly with a rubber spatula. Set aside. Let cool completely.

Place the cream cheese, peanut butter, granulated sugar, and vanilla in the bowl of an electric mixer. Beat on medium-low speed for 2 to 3 minutes, until ingredients are fully incorporated.

Pour the chocolate mixture into the peanut butter mixture and mix on low until just combined. Do not overmix. Spread evenly into the prepared crust. Refrigerate for 1 to 2 hours.

To make the topping, beat the cream to soft peaks in the clean bowl of an electric mixer. Add the confectioners' sugar and vanilla and beat until medium peaks form. Spoon the whipped cream into a pastry bag fitted with a large star tip. Pipe the cream decoratively over the top of the pie. Garnish with the grated chocolate and peanuts before serving.

summer fruit hand pies

As kids we used to buy individual hand pies at convenience stores when we stopped for gas on road trips. Hand pies are small pastry triangles filled with seasonal fruit that bake up quickly. Like the name says, you hold them in your hand—no plates or fork necessary—so just grab 'em and go.

MAKES 12 PIES

PASTRY

2 cups all-purpose flour

1 teaspoon kosher salt

½ pound (2 sticks) cold unsalted butter, cut into small cubes

FILLING

2 tablespoons unsalted butter

¼ cup sugar

1 cup blackberries

1½ cups blueberries

1 cup raspberries

2 peaches, peeled and thinly sliced

3 tablespoons all-purpose flour

¼ teaspoon ground cinnamon

2 eggs beaten with 1 tablespoon water for egg wash

2 tablespoons sugar

To make the pastry, place the flour and salt in a food processor and pulse 3 or 4 times to mix. Add the butter to the flour mixture through the feed tube. Pulse 6 to 8 times, until the mixture resembles coarse meal. With the machine running, slowly add ¼ cup ice water, pulsing until the mixture just holds together.

Remove the dough from the machine. Press it together into a ball and then flatten it into a small disk. Wrap the dough in plastic wrap and refrigerate for 1 hour.

To make the filling, melt the butter and sugar together in a saucepan. Add the blackberries, blueberries, raspberries, peaches, flour, and cinnamon. Simmer, stirring frequently so that the fruit doesn't burn, until the mixture is thick, about 10 minutes. Remove the saucepan from the heat and let cool.

Preheat the oven to 350°F. Line two baking sheets with parchment paper.

Roll out the dough on a lightly floured surface to a ⅛-inch thickness. Cut the dough into six 5-inch squares.

Place a heaping tablespoon of the fruit filling in the center of a square. Moisten the edges of the square with egg wash and fold into a triangle, pressing the edges to seal. Using a spatula, transfer the hand pie to the lined baking sheet and press the tines of a fork around the edges to seal. Repeat with the remaining squares, leaving 1 inch between the squares on the baking sheet. Gather and reroll the dough to make 6 more squares. Refrigerate for 20 minutes.

Brush the triangles with the egg wash and sprinkle with the sugar. Bake until the pies are golden, about 30 minutes. Transfer the pies to wire racks to cool before serving.

burnzie's coconut layer cake

As a proper Southern lady, my grandmother wanted to be called Mother Burns, not Grandma, by her grandchildren. That was quite a mouthful for some of us, so over time she became Burnzie. She was also a fine Southern cook and baked this coconut layer cake for just about every family gathering. I remember how she clamped a hand-cranked grinder to the edge of the counter to shave the fresh coconut. When she sprinkled the shaved coconut on top of the frosted cake, she called it snow. She decorated this cake for every holiday. I can remember that for Easter dinner she topped the cake with colorful jelly beans.

Burnzie had an all-white kitchen with bright red Formica countertops. When we arrived for dinner and went into the kitchen through a swinging door, the first thing we saw was this all-white dessert on a white cake pedestal against the red Formica. Everyone *ooh*ed and *ah*ed and said that the cake was just too beautiful to eat. But, of course, we did!

MAKES 10 TO 12 SERVINGS

CAKE

2¾ cups all-purpose flour

1 teaspoon baking powder

½ teaspoon baking soda

½ teaspoon kosher salt, plus a pinch

1¾ cups sugar

½ pound (2 sticks) unsalted butter, at
    room temperature

1 15-ounce can cream of coconut, such as
    Coco Lopez

4 large eggs, separated

1 tablespoon pure vanilla extract

1 cup buttermilk

SEVEN-MINUTE FROSTING

1½ cups sugar

4 large egg whites

½ teaspoon cream of tartar

⅛ teaspoon kosher salt

1 tablespoon pure vanilla extract

4 cups shredded sweetened coconut

½ cup jelly beans (optional)

Preheat the oven to 350°F. Butter and flour two 9 x 2-inch round cake pans.

To make the cake, whisk together the flour, baking powder, baking soda, and salt in a medium bowl. Combine the sugar, butter, and cream of coconut in a large bowl and beat with an electric mixer until light and fluffy. Beat in the egg yolks and vanilla. With the mixer on low, beat in the flour mixture and then the buttermilk, just until blended.

Wash and dry the beaters. In a separate large bowl, beat the egg whites with a pinch of salt until stiff but not dry. Carefully fold the beaten egg whites into the batter. Divide the batter between the prepared pans. Bake the layers until a tester inserted into the centers of the layers comes out clean, about 45 minutes. Cool the layers in the pans on a wire rack for 10 minutes. Run a small sharp knife around the edges of the pans to loosen the layers. Turn the layers out onto the rack and allow them to cool completely.

To make the frosting, clip a candy thermometer to the side of a saucepan. Put the sugar and ½ cup water in the saucepan and heat until the candy thermometer reads 240°F.

Put the egg whites, cream of tartar, and salt in the bowl of an electric mixer. Beat on low speed just until the egg whites are frothy. Slowly pour in the hot sugar mixture. Gradually increase the speed to high, beating until the mixture holds stiff peaks, for 7 minutes. Add the vanilla. Cover and chill the frosting in the refrigerator until ready to use, up to 4 hours in advance.

To assemble the cake, place one cake layer on a plate. Spread with 1 cup of the frosting and sprinkle with 1 cup of the shredded coconut. Top with the second cake layer and spread the remaining frosting over the top and sides of the cake. Sprinkle the remaining 3 cups coconut over the cake, gently pressing it into the sides to adhere. Garnish with the jelly beans, if using. (The cake can be assembled up to 1 day ahead. Cover with plastic wrap and refrigerate. Let the cake stand at room temperature for 2 hours before serving.)

pineapple upside-down cake

Flipping this cake from upside down to right side up is really dramatic, making this luscious cake fun to make and to present. While red maraschino cherries are a traditional decoration, use red and green ones when baking this for the Christmas holidays. The easiest way to bake this cake is in an ovenproof or cast-iron skillet. The turnout will be a breeze, and the presentation beautiful.

MAKES 8 SERVINGS

Vegetable oil spray

TOPPING

6 tablespoons unsalted butter

¾ cup packed light brown sugar

1 20-ounce can pineapple slices, drained and juice reserved

Maraschino cherries

CAKE

1½ cups all-purpose flour

2 teaspoons baking powder

¼ teaspoon kosher salt

6 tablespoons unsalted butter, at room temperature

1 cup granulated sugar

2 large eggs

1 teaspoon pure vanilla extract

1 15.5-ounce can crushed pineapple

½ cup unsweetened pineapple juice

Put one rack in the middle of the oven. Preheat the oven to 350°F. Spray a 10-inch ovenproof skillet with the vegetable oil spray.

To make the topping, melt the butter and brown sugar in a saucepan over medium heat until the sugar dissolves and the mixture is bubbly, 3 to 4 minutes. Pour the mixture into the prepared skillet. Arrange the pineapple slices on top of the sugar mixture, overlapping pieces slightly if needed. Place the cherries in the middle of the pineapple rings.

To make the cake, sift together the flour, baking powder, and salt.

Put the butter and sugar in the bowl of an electric mixer. Beat until light and fluffy, about 5 minutes. Add the eggs, one at a time, beating well after each addition. Beat in the vanilla. Add half of the flour mixture and beat on low speed just until blended. Add the pineapple and pineapple juice and beat to combine. Add the remaining flour mixture, beating just until blended.

Pour the batter evenly over the pineapple topping in the skillet and spread evenly. Bake the cake for about 45 minutes, or until golden on top and a tester inserted into the center of the cake comes out clean. Remove from the oven and let the cake cool for 5 minutes. Place a plate large enough to hold the cake facedown on top of the skillet. With the plate and skillet firmly pressed together, invert the cake onto the plate. Replace any pineapples or cherries stuck to the bottom of skillet. Serve the cake warm or at room temperature.

mimi's lemon pound cake

Oh, talk about tradition! This moist and lemony cake was my grandmother Mimi's signature dessert; she baked it whenever the family gathered. Made with plenty of lemon zest, lemon juice, and lemon curd (look for it where jams and jellies are sold if you don't want to make your own), there's plenty of pucker in every bite.

MAKES 10 TO 12 SERVINGS

Vegetable oil spray
Flour for dusting

CAKE

⅓ cup sour cream
⅓ cup store-bought lemon curd
1 tablespoon pure vanilla extract
3 cups all-purpose flour
¾ teaspoon baking powder
¾ teaspoon baking soda
¾ teaspoon kosher salt

¾ pound (3 sticks) unsalted butter, at
    room temperature
2¼ cups sugar
¼ cup finely grated lemon zest
5 large eggs
8 drops yellow food coloring (optional)

LEMON SYRUP

1 tablespoon finely grated lemon zest
⅓ cup fresh lemon juice

1 cup confectioners' sugar

Put one rack in the middle of the oven. Preheat the oven to 325°F. Spray a 12-cup Bundt pan with vegetable oil spray and dust with flour.

To make the cake, whisk together the sour cream, lemon curd, and vanilla in a bowl. Into another bowl, sift together the flour, baking powder, baking soda, and salt.

Cream the butter, sugar, and lemon zest together in the bowl of an electric mixer, until the mixture is light and fluffy. Add the eggs, one at a time, beating well after each addition. Add the food coloring (if using). Add the flour mixture alternately with the sour cream mixture, beginning and ending with the flour mixture and beating the batter after each addition until it is just combined.

Pour and evenly spread the batter into the prepared pan. Bake for 1 hour to 1 hour and 30 minutes, or until the cake is golden and a tester inserted into the center of the cake comes out clean. Let the cake cool in the pan on a wire rack for 20 minutes. Invert the cake onto a serving platter and carefully remove the pan.

To make the syrup while the cake is cooling, combine the lemon zest, lemon juice, and sugar in a saucepan over medium heat. Cook until the sugar is dissolved. Remove the syrup from the heat.

With a toothpick or fork, poke holes all over the cake. Pour three quarters of the lemon syrup over the cake. Pour some of the remaining syrup on each slice of the cake before serving.

carrot cake
with coconut cream cheese frosting

I decided to give my carrot cake a unique flavor boost by adding pineapple. For the frosting, which uses canned cream of coconut, don't shake the can before opening it. Open the can and, using a spoon, remove the thick coconut cream on top, leaving the thin milk on the bottom. It will measure three-quarters cup, just the right amount for making the frosting.

MAKES 12 SERVINGS

CAKE

2⅔ cup all-purpose flour

1 cup flaked sweetened coconut

2½ teaspoons ground cinnamon

2½ teaspoons baking powder

½ teaspoon baking soda

¾ teaspoon salt

2 cups sugar

1 cup vegetable oil

2 teaspoons pure vanilla extract

4 large eggs

4 cups grated carrots

2 8-ounce cans crushed pineapple, well drained

CREAM CHEESE FROSTING

2 8-ounce packages cream cheese, at room temperature

8 tablespoons (1 stick) unsalted butter, room temperature

¾ cup coconut cream from 1 15-ounce can cream of coconut (see headnote)

1 teaspoon pure vanilla extract

1½ cups confectioners' sugar

¼ cup flaked sweetened coconut, toasted

Preheat oven to 350°F. Grease a 9 x 13-inch baking pan.

To make the cake, put the flour, coconut, cinnamon, baking powder, baking soda, and salt in a medium bowl. Stir well to combine. Set aside.

Put the sugar, oil, and vanilla in the bowl of an electric mixer and blend until well combined. Add the eggs one at a time, blending well after each addition. On low speed, add the dry ingredients until they are fully incorporated, stopping the machine to scrape down the sides with a spatula. Fold in the carrots and crushed pineapple.

Pour the batter into the prepared pan. Bake for 50 to 55 minutes, until a tester inserted into the center of the cake comes out clean. Cool the cake in the pan on a wire rack for 2 hours.

To make the frosting, put the cream cheese and butter in the bowl of an electric mixer and beat until smooth. Add the coconut cream and vanilla and mix until completely incorporated. Add the confectioners' sugar and mix until creamy. Cover and refrigerate until the frosting is firm enough to spread, about 30 minutes. Spread a thick layer of the frosting on the top of the cake. Sprinkle on the toasted coconut before slicing and serving.

flourless chocolate cake

When we asked QVC's customers what kinds of dishes they'd like to see on my show, the response was, "More gluten-free desserts!" I wanted a chocolate (of course) dessert that bakers could proudly serve to everyone gathered around the table, whether on a gluten-free diet or not. Why single anyone out? This cake is a home run.

MAKES 6 TO 8 SERVINGS

Vegetable oil spray

1 pound (about 2⅔ cups) semisweet
   chocolate chips

8 tablespoons (1 stick) unsalted butter

1 teaspoon pure vanilla extract

8 large eggs, separated

¾ cup sugar

Preheat the oven to 350°F. Grease a 9-inch springform pan with the vegetable oil spray, then line the pan bottom with parchment paper.

Put the chocolate chips, butter, and vanilla in the top of a double boiler and set aside. Fill the bottom pan with 2 inches of water and bring to a boil. Reduce the heat to a simmer and place the chocolate mixture on top to melt, stirring occasionally.

Put the egg yolks and sugar in the bowl of an electric mixer and beat on medium speed until the mixture is light yellow and ribbonlike, about 6 minutes.

Whisk ½ cup of the chocolate mixture into the egg yolk mixture to temper the eggs. Then, whisk in the rest of the chocolate mixture.

In a clean mixing bowl, beat the egg whites until stiff peaks form. Using a spatula, fold the egg whites into the batter until no white streaks remain.

Pour the batter into the prepared pan. Bake for 45 to 55 minutes, until the cake is set or the top is cracked and a toothpick inserted into the center comes out with moist crumbs. Let stand for 10 minutes, then remove the springform from the cake. (The cake may be made a day ahead, covered, and refrigerated. Bring to room temperature before serving.)

dishin' with DAVID

EVERYTHING EGGS ARE CRACKED UP TO BE

To guarantee that your eggs will deliver lightness and leavening to your baking.

- Separate eggs when they're cold, right from the refrigerator.
- Let the whites sit at room temperature for 30 minutes before whipping for greater volume.

three-layer chocolate cake
with chocolate frosting

There are three things I love about this dessert: It has chocolate, chocolate, and even more chocolate. The cake is made with three rich chocolate layers and a smooth and creamy chocolate frosting. The secret ingredient is coffee, which enhances the cocoa's flavor and results in a more chocolaty cake. If other desserts are called "death by chocolate," then this one should certainly be called "heaven by chocolate."

MAKES 12 TO 14 SERVINGS

CAKE

2½ cups all-purpose flour

1½ cups unsweetened cocoa powder (not Dutch process)

2 teaspoons baking soda

1 teaspoon baking powder

1¼ teaspoons kosher salt

¾ cup vegetable oil

3 cups sugar

3 large eggs

1½ teaspoons pure vanilla extract

1½ cups buttermilk

1½ cups warm brewed coffee

CHOCOLATE FROSTING

1 pound dark chocolate (60% cacao), finely chopped

1 pound (about 2⅔ cups) semisweet chocolate chips

2 cups heavy cream

½ cup light corn syrup

Preheat the oven to 350°F. Butter three 9 x 2-inch round cake pans and line the bottoms with parchment. Butter the parchment.

To make the cake, sift together the flour, cocoa powder, baking soda, baking powder, and salt in a bowl. Set aside. Combine the vegetable oil, sugar, eggs, and vanilla in the bowl of an electric mixer and beat until creamy and light. Add one third of the dry ingredients, followed by one third of the buttermilk and one third of the coffee. Mix to combine. Repeat the additions twice, stopping the mixer as necessary to scrape down the sides of the bowl. Beat until smooth.

Divide the batter evenly among the prepared pans and bake for 40 to 50 minutes, until a tester inserted into the centers of the layers comes out clean. Cool the layers in the pans on a wire rack for 30 minutes. Run a small sharp knife around the edges of the pans and invert the layers onto the racks. Carefully remove the parchment and cool the layers completely. (Cake layers may be made 1 day ahead and kept, wrapped well in plastic wrap, at room temperature.)

To make the frosting, place the chopped chocolate and chocolate chips in a bowl. Bring the cream and corn syrup to a boil in a saucepan. As soon as the mixture comes to a boil, pour it into the bowl with the chocolate and whisk until the chocolate is melted. Let cool for 10 to 15 minutes, until spreadable. (The frosting may be covered and refrigerated, but return it to room temperature before using.)

Place one cake layer on a plate and spread with a layer of frosting. Add a second cake layer and another layer of frosting. Top with the third cake layer and spread the remaining frosting over the top and sides of the cake. (The cake will keep, covered and refrigerated, for up to 3 days. Bring to room temperature before serving.)

dishin' with DAVID ||| THE ICING ON THE CAKE

When Cake Boss Buddy Valastro was on the show, he said, "Homemade cakes often look unprofessional because most people put on the icing while the cake layers are still warm, so the icing runs. Put the cake layers in the refrigerator or freezer so they become somewhat stiff and easier to work with. Then, once the cake is iced, put it back in the fridge. Take it out when the icing is a little stiff, and use a wet knife to get a perfectly smooth top and sides."

german chocolate cupcakes

German chocolate cake is one of my favorite desserts, but it's such a big cake and somewhat messy to serve. Here's a great solution: Make German chocolate cupcakes instead. They're easier to eat and help with portion control, but the flavor and moistness are right there down to the last crumb. One note: Using hot tap water in the batter is essential.

MAKES 12 CUPCAKES

CUPCAKES

1½ cups all-purpose flour

¼ cup unsweetened cocoa powder (not Dutch process)

1¼ teaspoons baking soda

½ teaspoon salt

⅓ cup vegetable oil

¾ cup granulated sugar

¼ cup packed light brown sugar

2 large eggs, at room temperature

1½ teaspoons pure vanilla extract

⅔ cup sour cream

⅔ cup hot tap water

FROSTING

1 14-ounce can sweetened condensed milk

8 tablespoons (1 stick) unsalted butter

2 large egg yolks

7 ounces (heaping ¾ cup) semisweet chocolate chips

1 cup toasted and chopped pecans

1½ cups shredded sweetened coconut

2 teaspoons pure vanilla extract

Preheat the oven to 350°F. Line a standard 12-cup muffin pan with paper muffin cups.

To make the cupcakes, whisk together the flour, cocoa powder, baking soda, and salt in a medium bowl. Combine the oil, granulated sugar, brown sugar, eggs, vanilla, and sour cream in a medium bowl and mix until all ingredients are combined. Add the dry ingredients to the wet ingredients and mix well. Add the hot tap water and mix until all the ingredients are fully incorporated.

Divide the batter among the muffin cups, filling each cup to the top. Bake, rotating the pan halfway through, for 25 to 30 minutes, until a tester inserted into the center of a cupcake comes out clean. Transfer the muffin pan to a wire rack and cool for 10 minutes. Turn the cupcakes out onto the wire rack and allow them to cool completely.

To make the frosting, combine the condensed milk, butter, and egg yolks in a medium saucepan. Cook over medium heat, stirring frequently, 6 to 7 minutes. Add the chocolate chips and stir until completely melted. Remove the saucepan from the heat. Stir in the pecans, coconut, and vanilla. Let the mixture cool for 30 to 40 minutes.

Spread the frosting on the cupcakes and serve. Cupcakes can be stored in an airtight container for up to 3 days.

banana pudding cheesecake

Oh my word, I don't even want to think about how much banana pudding I ate as a kid. Everyone—Mom, my grandmothers, and aunts—made her own version of this dessert. A clear glass pedestal bowl was lined with Nilla Wafers and then the pudding was spooned in and chilled. Because I'm such a fan of this pudding, as well as cheesecake, I asked myself, "Why not put the two together and bake them?" This is a very rich dessert, so you may want to serve small portions. That means a bigger slice for me!

MAKES 10 TO 12 SERVINGS

CRUST
1½ cups finely crushed vanilla wafer cookies, such as Nilla Wafers

6 tablespoons unsalted butter, melted

¼ cup sugar

1 teaspoon ground cinnamon

FILLING
2 8-ounce packages cream cheese, at room temperature

¾ cup sugar

2 teaspoons fresh lemon juice

4 large eggs

1 cup (8 ounces) sour cream

1 teaspoon banana extract

1 cup mashed very ripe bananas (about 3 bananas)

1 banana, sliced

Preheat the oven to 350°F. Butter a 9-inch round springform pan.

To make the crust, in a medium bowl, stir together the crumbs with the butter, sugar, and cinnamon. Press the mixture evenly over the bottom and partially up the sides of the prepared pan. Bake for about 10 minutes, until golden brown. Let the crust cool on a wire rack.

To make the filling, combine the cream cheese, sugar, and lemon juice in the bowl of an electric mixer and beat until smooth, scraping down the sides of the bowl as necessary. Add the eggs, one at a time, beating well after each addition. Scrape down the sides of the bowl and stir in the sour cream, banana extract, and mashed bananas.

Pour the banana mixture into the prepared crust. Bake for 1 hour, or until the center is set and firm. Turn off the oven and open the door. Allow the cheesecake to cool to room temperature in the oven. Cover with plastic wrap and refrigerate for at least 2 hours before serving. Garnish with banana slices.

peach cobbler

Every summer when the Venable family hit the road for vacation, we'd stop and buy fresh peaches at a roadside stand. We'd eat our fill and bring the rest to friends and family for peach cobblers. My recipe is easy and always brings smiles. Be sure to use the freshest and ripest summer peaches that you can find.

MAKES 8 SERVINGS

8 tablespoons (1 stick) unsalted butter, at
room temperature

PEACHES
8 to 10 peaches, peeled, pitted, and thinly
sliced
½ cup sugar
½ teaspoon ground cinnamon

¼ teaspoon ground nutmeg
Juice of ½ lemon
2 teaspoons cornstarch

BATTER
1 cup all-purpose flour
1 cup sugar
2 teaspoons baking powder
¼ teaspoon kosher salt

¾ cup milk
1 large egg
1 teaspoon pure vanilla extract

2 to 3 tablespoons sugar
1 pint vanilla ice cream

Preheat the oven to 350°F. Put the butter in a 9 x 13-inch baking dish and place in the oven to melt. Once melted, remove from the oven. Keep the oven on.

To make the peaches, combine the sliced peaches, sugar, cinnamon, nutmeg, lemon juice, and cornstarch in a bowl and toss well. Set aside.

To make the batter, combine the flour, sugar, baking powder, and salt in a bowl. Stir in the milk, egg, and vanilla. Pour the batter over the melted butter.

Arrange the peach slices on top of the batter. Sprinkle the remaining sugar over the entire cobbler. Bake for 25 to 30 minutes, until the top is golden brown and the cake begins to pull away from the sides of the baking dish. Remove to a wire rack to cool for 10 minutes before serving. Spoon a scoop of ice cream over each serving.

apple crisp

A family trip to an apple orchard is an adventure your kids will remember for years. Pack a picnic lunch and take a hayride to the trees farthest from the parking lot—that's where you'll find the best fruit. At home, this warm-from-the-oven apple crisp quickly goes together for that evening's dessert. Oh, don't forget to put a scoop of vanilla ice cream on each serving. Can't you just smell the love?

MAKES 6 SERVINGS

TOPPING

12 tablespoons (1½ sticks) unsalted butter, at room temperature

1½ cups packed brown sugar

1½ cups all-purpose flour

1½ cups quick-cooking oats

1½ teaspoons pure vanilla extract

1½ teaspoons ground cinnamon

¼ teaspoon ground nutmeg

FILLING

⅓ cup granulated sugar

1 tablespoon all-purpose flour

2 tablespoons fresh lemon juice

1½ teaspoons pure vanilla extract

2 teaspoons ground cinnamon

¼ teaspoon ground nutmeg

4 Granny Smith apples, peeled, cored, and sliced ¼ inch thick

4 Honey Crisp apples, peeled, cored and sliced ¼ inch thick

Preheat the oven to 350°F.

To prepare the topping, put the butter and brown sugar into the bowl of an electric mixer. Cream until light and fluffy, about 5 minutes. Add the flour, oats, vanilla, cinnamon, and nutmeg and mix until the dough becomes crumbly. Do not overmix. Set aside.

To prepare the filling, combine the sugar, flour, lemon juice, vanilla, cinnamon, and nutmeg in a bowl. Add the apple slices and toss to coat.

Place the apple mixture in a 9 x 13-inch baking dish. Sprinkle the topping evenly over the apples. Bake for 35 to 45 minutes, until the topping is golden brown and the apples are tender when pierced with a fork. Set on a wire rack to cool a bit before serving warm.

skillet apples
with cranberries

Nothing feels more like home than fresh apples bubbling on the stove top. Butter and brown sugar make each apple slice glisten, and the cranberries provide the perfect tartness and beautiful color. Serve this as a dessert during autumn and the winter months or as the ideal side dish with Mustard-Glazed Rosemary Pork Tenderloins (page 132).

MAKES 6 SERVINGS

6 large cooking apples, such as Granny Smiths, peeled, cored, and sliced ¼ inch thick

1 tablespoon fresh lemon juice

1 tablespoon cornstarch

4 tablespoons (½ stick) unsalted butter

⅓ cup packed dark brown sugar

½ teaspoon ground cinnamon

Pinch of ground nutmeg

¼ cup dried cranberries

Whipped cream

Toss the apple slices with the lemon juice in a medium bowl and set aside. In a small bowl, whisk together the cornstarch and ½ cup water until there are no lumps. Set aside.

Melt the butter in a large skillet over medium heat. Add the brown sugar and apple slices and sauté, stirring constantly, until the apples are tender and just beginning to turn golden, 6 to 8 minutes. Stir in the cornstarch mixture. Stir in the cinnamon and nutmeg, add the cranberries, and bring the mixture to a simmer. Simmer, stirring occasionally, until the sauce has thickened, 3 to 5 minutes. Serve warm with a dollop of whipped cream.

super chunky chocolate chip cookies

Ask anyone what their favorite homemade cookie is, and chances are good that the answer will be chocolate chip. If you're going to make these from scratch, you should do them up right. They should have plenty of chocolate chips *and* chocolate chunks, sugar, and butter, and be slightly underbaked. The only thing left is to pour a glass of cold milk to wash them down.

MAKES 24 COOKIES

2¼ cups all-purpose flour

1 teaspoon kosher salt

¾ teaspoon baking soda

½ teaspoon baking powder

¾ cup (1½ sticks) unsalted butter, at room temperature

1 cup packed light brown sugar

½ cup granulated sugar

2 large eggs

1½ teaspoons pure vanilla extract

8 ounces dark chocolate, cut into ½-inch or smaller chunks

8 ounces (about 1½ cups) semisweet chocolate chips

Preheat the oven to 350°F. Line two baking sheets with silicone mats or parchment paper.

Sift the flour, salt, baking soda, and baking powder together into a medium bowl. Set aside.

Beat the butter, brown sugar, and granulated sugar in the bowl of an electric mixer until light and fluffy, about 5 minutes. Add the eggs, one at a time, beating well after each addition. Beat in the vanilla. Add the flour mixture and beat until combined. Using a spatula, fold in the chocolate chunks and chips.

Form 2-ounce balls, and flatten halfway.

Bake for 14 to 15 minutes, rotating the baking sheets halfway through the baking time, just until slightly underdone and light golden brown on the outside edges. Let the cookies cool on the baking sheets.

apple-cinnamon snickerdoodles

What a funny name for a cookie! These old-fashioned cinnamon sugar cookies are crackled on the outside but soft on the inside. I dress up my snickerdoodles by adding some chopped Granny Smith apples to the batter, which also makes them moist. These are fun cookies to bake with your kids. Make a double batch. These are certain to shake up your next bake sale.

MAKES 18 COOKIES

COOKIES

3¼ cups all-purpose flour

3 tablespoons cornstarch

1½ teaspoons baking soda

1 teaspoon ground cinnamon

¾ teaspoon ground nutmeg

¾ teaspoon kosher salt

12 tablespoons (1½ sticks) unsalted butter, at room temperature

1 cup packed light brown sugar

1 cup granulated sugar

3 large eggs

2 medium Granny Smith apples, peeled, cored, and cut into ¼-inch chunks

TOPPING

½ cup granulated sugar

1 tablespoon ground cinnamon

Preheat the oven to 350°F. Line two baking sheets with silicone mats or parchment paper.

To make the cookies, sift together the flour, cornstarch, baking soda, cinnamon, nutmeg, and salt into a large bowl.

Cream the butter in the bowl of an electric mixer, until light and fluffy, about 3 minutes. Add the brown sugar and granulated sugar and mix until fully incorporated. Add the eggs, one at a time, beating well after each addition. Gradually add the flour mixture in three additions, beating well after each addition. Using a spatula, fold in the apples.

To make the topping, combine the granulated sugar and cinnamon on a large plate.

Measure a heaping tablespoon of the dough and roll it into a ball between clean hands. Roll the ball in the cinnamon-sugar mixture, coating it on all sides. Repeat with the remaining dough. Arrange the balls on the prepared baking sheets, spacing them 2 inches apart. Flatten each ball slightly with your fingers.

Bake the cookies for 18 to 20 minutes, rotating the baking sheets from top to bottom and front to back once after 9 minutes, until they are golden and just barely set. Let the cookies cool on the baking sheets for 10 minutes. Transfer the cookies to wire racks to cool.

chocolate–peanut butter brownies

My all-time favorite dessert combination is chocolate and peanut butter, so I've included a pie (page 216) and these brownies with those classic flavors. Chances are good that you've got all the necessary ingredients in your pantry, so you can quickly make these treats for tomorrow's bridge game or tonight's dessert.

MAKES 12 BROWNIES

BROWNIES

2 ounces unsweetened chocolate

8 tablespoons (1 stick) unsalted butter, diced

2 large eggs

1 cup granulated sugar

1 teaspoon pure vanilla extract

½ cup all-purpose flour

PEANUT BUTTER FILLING

1½ cups confectioners' sugar

½ cup creamy peanut butter

4 tablespoons (½ stick) unsalted butter, at room temperature

2 to 3 tablespoons half-and-half, heavy cream, or milk

GLAZE

1 ounce semisweet chocolate

1 tablespoon unsalted butter

Preheat the oven to 350°F. Butter and flour a 9 x 2-inch square cake pan.

To make the brownies, melt the chocolate and butter in a small saucepan over low heat. Set aside. Beat the eggs and sugar in the bowl of an electric mixer until light and fluffy, about 2 minutes. Beat in the vanilla. Stir in the flour and the melted chocolate mixture.

Pour the batter into the prepared pan and bake for about 25 minutes, until a tester inserted into the center of the brownies comes out with a few moist crumbs attached. Cool the brownies on a wire rack for 15 minutes.

To make the filling, combine the confectioners' sugar, peanut butter, and butter in the bowl of an electric mixer and beat until smooth. Stir in the half-and-half a little at a time until the mixture reaches spreading consistency. Spread the peanut butter filling evenly over the brownies, cover, and chill until firm.

To make the glaze, melt the chocolate and butter in a small saucepan over low heat, stirring until smooth. Drizzle the glaze over the brownies and chill until set, about 1 hour. Cut the brownies into squares and store them in an airtight container in the refrigerator.

bananas foster bread pudding

If you've ever ordered bananas Foster in a fancy restaurant, you know the server puts on quite a performance. The bananas and brown sugar are cooked in a sauté pan. Then liqueur is added to the pan, dramatically ignited with a match, and ka-boom—the flames leap up. Once the flames die down, the warm mixture is poured over ice cream and set before you. I don't know anyone who has the time to do this at home, but having enjoyed this classic many times, I wanted to combine these flavors in a make-ahead bread pudding. Serve this rich, grown-up dessert at your next dinner party.

MAKES 6 TO 8 SERVINGS

BREAD PUDDING

1½ French baguette loaves, cut into 1-inch slices

3 cups milk

½ cup heavy cream

3 tablespoons unsalted butter, melted

5 large eggs, lightly beaten

2 tablespoons dark rum

1 tablespoon banana liqueur

1 teaspoon pure vanilla extract

1 cup granulated sugar

½ teaspoon ground cinnamon

3 very ripe bananas, mashed

SAUCE

5 tablespoons unsalted butter

1 cup packed light brown sugar

½ teaspoon ground cinnamon

2 tablespoons banana liqueur

4 ripe bananas, peeled and sliced

⅓ cup dark rum

Vanilla ice cream

Preheat the oven to 400°F.

To make the bread pudding, spread the bread slices on a baking sheet and bake until dry and lightly toasted, about 10 minutes. Remove the bread from the oven and set aside. Turn off the oven.

Whisk together the milk, cream, butter, eggs, rum, banana liqueur, and vanilla in a large bowl. Add the sugar and cinnamon and whisk to blend. Add the bread cubes and stir until well coated. Cover the bowl with plastic wrap and refrigerate the mixture for 3 hours, until the bread has absorbed most of the liquid.

Preheat the oven to 350°F.

Remove the mixture from the refrigerator and stir in the mashed bananas. Spread the mixture into a 3½-quart baking dish. Bake, uncovered, for 50 minutes to 1 hour, until a knife inserted into the center of the pudding comes out clean.

To make the sauce, heat the butter, brown sugar, and cinnamon in a medium skillet over low heat. Cook, stirring constantly, until the sugar dissolves. Stir in the banana liqueur and banana slices. Continue to cook until the bananas soften and begin to brown. Add the rum and carefully ignite the mixture with a long match. Cook until the flame dies out and the mixture is syrupy, 1 to 2 minutes. Remove the skillet from the heat.

Spoon the bread pudding into individual bowls. Top each serving with a scoop of vanilla ice cream and a drizzle of the sauce.

acknowledgments

Special heartfelt thanks to my family for their support and love, especially my mother, Sarah, my sister, Jackie, and my brother, Chip. Additional gratitude goes to my niece Hannah and my nephew Preston and my other family members who shaped my love of food, my late father, Jon, my late grandmother Mimi, and my late grandmother Burnzie.

My close friends and loved ones who cheered me through this entire process: Tara, Gail, Mr. Raleighs, John, Kevin, Ed, Jill, Lenny, Michael and Jane (Honey). To Jimmy D'Angelo for your constant support, concern, and encouragement. You have never stopped believing in me … I am a better person because of you!

My *In the Kitchen with David* support crew, Jonathan Dowdell, Mary DeAngelis, Lori Leone, Christa Bukowski, Amy Lucas, Joe Pascavage, Ani Manouchehri, Wes Weisser, Mariann Shumbo, and Gabe Steiner. There would be no show and no cookbook without your unbelievable dedication and support.

My editor, Pamela Cannon, who made this project run smoothly with her guidance and her direction. You and the other members of the Ballantine team made this effort effortless.

My friend Harriet Bell, who helped me find my "voice" and saw to it that my book made sense from beginning to end. Your patience, knowledge, and dedication inspire me.

My photographer, Ben Fink, brought the book to life with his stunning photographs. Your friendship is a treasure to me.

My creative director, Peter Browne, is a force of nature! Your endless talent and focus made this book so special. I'm grateful everyday that you found your way to QVC.

My culinary team at QVC who partnered with me to make the recipes sing. Thanks to Paula Bower, James Davignon, Andrea Schwob, Lynn Willis, Scott Hebert, Jill Schoenfeld, Michele Pilone, Rochelle Quirple, Mitch Meshon, Lisa Ventura, Carole Haffey, Jeri Estok, Bonne DiTomo, John Burwell, Brenda Wolf, Brad Rust, Ryan Sulikowski, Nick DiCiurcio, and Phil Falsone.

The people who graciously allowed us to take photographs in their stores, including Tim Anson at The Fresh Market, Glen Mills, Pennsylvania; Chris Hill at Hill's Quality Seafood Market, Inc.; and Dan and Dorothy Boxler at Country Butcher Fine Foods Market. My gratitude to Wes Weisser for the great photograph of Paula Deen and me.

Special thanks to Mariellen Ward for her tireless efforts in coordinating photography and keeping me well fed in the process!

My project leader, Carol Snyder, who worked with this entire endeavor from beginning to end. Thanks for your day-to-day attention and support in making all the elements come together.

Our QVC management team that supported me throughout the entire project: Doug Rose, Karen Fonner, Tara Hunter, Jack Comstock, Scott Crossin, Angie Simmons, Claire Watts, and Mike George.

My right arm, Priscilla Millard, who made sure I stayed on schedule while spending hours autographing cookbooks. Your positive attitude is a blessing to me and I've found a friend for life in you!

My fellow QVC program hosts. Your support and encouragement mean the world to me. We are a true team and I value you all so much for your friendship and professionalism. Thanks for being the best in the business!

Our weekly *In the Kitchen with David* guests, who make every show special.

My dear friend Paula Deen, a big thank-you and hug for writing the Foreword to my book. Thanks for your friendship and the laughter over the years! I adore you!

Finally, and most important, to all the Foodies who watch *In the Kitchen with David* each week. Your loyalty and support make our show great! You all inspire me with your love of cooking and great food. You keep me going with your enthusiasm and excitement. We are truly one big Family of Foodies!

index

about the author

DAVID VENABLE joined QVC as a program host in 1993 and has since helped establish and build the multimedia retailer's gourmet food business. His hit show, *In the Kitchen with David,*® offers a unique interactive viewership experience and features the latest in gourmet foods, cookware, kitchen gadgets, and cookbooks. While not a chef, Venable, well known as QVC's Resident Foodie, loves to cook, and his passion revolves around all things food. Prior to joining QVC, Venable was an anchor/reporter for WOAY-TV in Oak Hill, West Virginia, and CBS-affiliate WTAJ-TV in Altoona, Pennsylvania. He earned his bachelor's degree from the University of North Carolina, Chapel Hill, and lives in Pennsylvania.